Growing the Next
Silicon Valley

Growing the Next Silicon Valley

A Guide for Successful Regional Planning

Roger Miller
University of Quebec

Marcel Côté
SECOR, Inc.

Lexington Books
D.C. Heath and Company/Lexington, Massachusetts/Toronto

This book's title first appeared in the *Harvard Business Review*. It is used with permission from "Growing the Next Silicon Valley," by Roger Miller and Marcel Côté, *Harvard Business Review*, July/August 1985.

Library of Congress Cataloging-in-Publication Data

Miller, Roger.
    Growing the next Silicon Valley.

    Bibliography: p.
    Includes index.
    1. Regional planning—United States 2. Regional economics. 3. High technology—
United States.
    I. Côté, Marcel. II. Title.
    HT392.M55 1987   338.973   86-45880
    ISBN 0-669-14577-7 (alk. paper)

Published simultaneously in Canada
Printed in the United States of America
Casebound International Standard Book Number: 0-669-14577-7
Library of Congress Catalog Card Number: 86-45880

The paper used in this publication meets the minimum requirements of American National Standard for Information Sciences—Permanence of Paper for Printed Library Materials, ANSI Z39.48-1984. ∞™

87 88 89 90 8 7 6 5 4 3 2 1

To
James F. Morgan,
whose idealism is only constrained
by his methodical realism

Contents

Figures and Tables

Figures

Tables

Preface

Honoré de Balzac captured exceptionally well the dynamics of economic development. In the "Médecin de Campagne," in 1813 the country doctor noted to his friend, Genestas, that economic development came to St. Laurent-du-Pont by the actions of local people and leaders who began to better exploit the resources at their disposal via new outside information. The doctor and Genestas showed local people how to make baskets, leather gear, and wood products. With increasing wealth, a veterinarian came to the town and eventually meat exportation became important. As wealth accumulated, a shoemaker, a hatter, and a tailor set up shops. After nineteen years, the doctor noted that trade of local products with nearby Grenoble led to further increases in economic wealth. Local tanneries imported leather from Provence and exported hats and leather products. Education became a good desired by all. Very soon, said the doctor, "we will decorate our church, have bourgeois houses and a public market."

The nature of economic development has not changed very much. But now instead of using steam machines to operate the lumber plant, we are likely to employ computer-aided manufacturing equipment. Such technology ensures an optimal cutting pattern, given the relative prices of chips and construction lumber products.

This book is about promoting economic development through high technology. This book evolved from two sources. The first was a university graduate-level course on the management of technology that emphasized the role that technology and management play in economic development. The course aimed to help students and executives formulate business plans for new ventures. The second inspiration was twenty-years worth of hands-on experience in economic development activities offered by business executives, entrepreneurs, and public officials, all committed to the economic development of their regions.

Studying the process of economic growth has dominated the field of political economy for many centuries. The origin of the wealth of nations has indeed been the main focus of inquiry of classical economists like Adam

Smith and John Ricardo. Institutional economists, like W. Sombart, J.A. Schumpeter, F. Perroux, and L. Dupriez, remained committed to understanding the entrepreneurial sources of economic growth. Only in the twentieth century did economists bring the focus mainly to problems associated with short-term equilibrium issues. However, in 1967, *The Economy of Cities* by Jane Jacobs was published, which rekindled the classical tradition of analyzing economic growth as a long-term process. This book dealt with the pivotal role of cities in the process of economic development. In particular, Jacobs stressed the importance of creative imports-substitution, the core of the development of growing cities. Her most recent book, *Cities and the Wealth of Nations,* elaborates on these views and, in particular, analyzes the role cities play in the growth of countries. It is now common to examine the conditions that encourage new economic activities. Many economists now believe that underemployment of resources is due to deficiencies in the regenerative process of economies rather than to short-term disequilibria, for which fiscal and monetary policies are appropriate.

Our approach to promoting economic growth puts a strong emphasis on its regional dimension, even in high technology industries. The spatial element is essential not only to economic activities, but also to the growth process. Growth potentials and economic structures vary considerably between regions. Large cities play a fundamental role in economic growth. In fact, it is mostly in large cities that new products and innovations develop. Thus, we firmly believe that any analysis of the process of economic growth should have a regional perspective.

The Plan of the Book

This book is divided into four parts and nine chapters. The first part provides an introduction and examines the geography of high technology in the United States. Chapter 1 outlines the core of our argument. Chapter 2 argues that although clusters may form in areas where leading-edge research is conducted, entrepreneurs will seize opportunities and rapidly diffuse the technology.

The second part outlines our conceptual framework. Chapter 3 describes the key characteristics of a high-technology cluster. The processes of "incubation," "role modeling," and "sponsorship" are explained in chapter 4. The institutional infrastructures that fuel the agglomeration and the entrepreneurial process are analyzed in chapter 5.

The third part uses case histories to illustrate two high-technology clusters. Chapter 6 provides a detailed history of the growth of high technology in the Twin Cities following World War II. Chapter 7 describes the resurgence of high technology in Philadelphia, a city hit hard by the loss of manufacturing jobs after the war.

The fourth part focuses on action programs designed by public–private partnerships to accelerate the growth of high technology in a region. Chapter 8 describes the mirages and pitfalls to avoid when planning a strategy. Chapter 9 outlines the key components of a long-term strategy that can guide players in the private, as well as the public, sectors.

Both Roger Miller and Marcel Côté are Fellows at the Center for International Affairs at Harvard University. Funding for a part of this research was made available by the University Consortium for Research on North America. Tom Haferd, a research assistant at the CFIA and director of the Elmbrook Center in Cambridge, Massachusetts, managed the data-gathering process and built the databank. Monique Prud'Homme survived our countless modifications and typed our manuscript with apparent effortlessness.

Part I
High Technology and Economic Development

High technology firms are sought-after commodities. Governments and business executives actively promote their development. Expectations are high, but the road towards high-technology development is indeed rocky. Not many regions have been successful at recreating a Silicon Valley, despite forceful public actions.

A realistic look at technology-intensive industries drives home a few sobering facts. First, high technology represents only a third of high-growth industries. Most high-growth industries are not related to high technology, whatever the definition. Second, even when high-technology industries exhibit substantial growth, they contribute only a minor fraction of a community's employment. Third, high-technology firms represent a small share of business activities. Although high-technology industries will grow more than twice as fast as all other business sectors over the next ten years, they will represent, at most, 6 percent of the overall economy in terms of sales and employment. Finally, few high-technology start-ups will become major competitors in growing industries; most will flounder or stagnate.

Chapter 1 introduces the theme that the clustering of high-technology firms is due to venturing activities of entrepreneurs and corporations who build on the regional infrastructure. Chapter 2 focuses on the widespread distribution of high-technology clusters in metropolitan areas.

1

The Development of High-Technology Clusters: An Introduction

The place is Mountain View in 1961. From the window of the third story of the new apartment complex, the view is clear toward the South. There are green fields all the way to the horizon. The air is clean. There are rows and rows of citrus and orange groves. San Jose is seventeen miles away to the South. Driving to San Jose at night is a lonely affair in the dark farming country.

Twenty-five years later, one of us who lived in that apartment went back to Mountain View. The apartment building was gone, and the view from there was now cluttered by rows and rows of roof tops. A typical, low-level industrial and commercial landscape had emerged, built by real estate developers to meet the demand for space. "For Rent" signs were everywhere. Between the bluff in Mountain View, where the apartment stood, and San Jose stands the new wonder of industrial America—Silicon Valley.

A few thousand people worked in the electronics industry in Santa Clara County (which extends from San Jose north to Menlo Park, north of Stanford University) when it all began. Great names of the U.S. computer and telecommunications industries—Hewlett-Packard, National Semiconductor, Intel, and the brightest star of them all, Apple Corporation—were born and grew up in the flat, sun-soaked valley. It all happened in about twenty-five years. Right after World War II, there was hardly anything but agricultural land around Stanford University and to the south toward San Jose. In 1980, when Silicon Valley attained its zenith, over 5,000 different high-technology companies were located in the area.

When one of us, Roger Miller, arrived at Stanford in 1961, no great inquiry was necessary to learn the University's pecking order. The core of Stanford University is the Quadrangle, or the "Quad" to the locals, a series of intercommunicating buildings laid out in a square. The park in the center meshed with the Spanish architecture. Bicycles were parked outside, of course. Most of the schools and the departments were housed here.

The electrical engineering department, a small but visible entity, occupied one building in the southwest corner. Electrical engineering (EE) was known as the toughest department. EE students knew it and bragged about it. Other students also knew it. The former president of the university was originally from the electrical engineering department. This was also well known.

The electrical engineering department was the best department at Stanford. Intentions were to make it the best in North America. More than the other departments and schools at Stanford, it was drawing "straight A" students from all over America.

Moreover, the EE department meant business. It became routine to graduate from the department and start a business. Professors were for it, so was the Dean. The President was so much for it that the University would lease land in Menlo Park, just north of the University to graduates if they needed it. This was part of the mystique of the EE department. Graduates Hewlet and Packard did it, the Varian Associates was also founded by Stanford alumni. Several other companies with unfamiliar names got their starts this way. Their founders came from the EE department, not from the business school.

In 1961, the industrial park in Menlo Park was by today's standards, small. But on campus, it was predicted that more businesses would come out of the EE department. And the industrial park would expand. The semiconductor technology was starting to be translated into products. Transistors were hot. Printed circuits were hot. Computer technology was progressing rapidly, although IBM had not yet arrived in the area.

Whether at that time students or professors foresaw the Silicon Valley of today will never be known. But the faith was there that something great would come out of Menlo Park and out of the semiconductor technology wave. Moreover, those who wanted to be part of this empire building experience were confident that they could be. This was the mood in Palo Alto in 1961.

Meanwhile, 3,000 miles away on the East Coast, in the Boston area, a similar phenomenon was developing—Route 128. Even today, just as in the early sixties, Route 128 does not project the image of high technology to the casual observer. Indeed, the image of Route 128 was built by the press and various authors. Route 128 is the name of a phenomenon. The phenomenon is the multiplication of high-technology firms in the beltway around Boston in the past thirty years.

The development of Route 128 differs greatly from that of Silicon Valley. The starting point was different. It was not a university. Indeed, MIT's electrical engineering department was losing personnel to Stanford. The impetus did not come from MIT. Venture capitalists, particularly "General" Doriot, are the folk heroes of Route 128. Military research, not the semiconductor revolution, provided the technological base for Route 128.

An Entrepreneurial Phenomenon

Despite the dissimilarities, the entrepreneurial process fueled the growth of both Silicon Valley and Route 128. The entrepreneurial process thrives on agglomeration effects and feeds back upon itself to sustain momentum. The process rests on start-up firms that exploit a new technology, and new specialized firms that service these technology-based companies. These firms grow at different rates. Some of them have become, in less than twenty years, multinational corporations perched high up on the "Fortune 500" list.

Yet, most high-technology firms remain small, with less than 100 employees. Some of them tap small-market niches. Others service the needs of larger, local high-technology establishments, as subcontractors and parts manufacturers. Branch plants of outside firms are established in the area, thus joining local firms. Acquisitions and mergers with smaller firms bring in the well-known companies.

High-technology firms are distributed throughout North America in several clusters. What makes high-technology firms agglomerate in specific areas? A complex process leads to the emergence of a cluster. Usually entrepreneurs nurture their own ventures while working in "incubator" firms, learning about the technology and marketplace and slowly developing their ideas. They are encouraged by the successes of other entrepreneurs. Entrepreneurs use the success next door to convince investors, bankers, suppliers, and key colleagues to join them in new ventures. Their first years are usually tough. Securing key clients is usually critical. The richer the commercial environment is for new firms, the easier it is for entrepreneurs to succeed.

The success of entrepreneurs improves the conditions for those who follow. Agglomeration effects take hold: incubators multiply, success stories abound, and the commercial environment is enriched by sponsoring organizations on the look-out for the specialized technologies of the new firms.

The search for leading-edge technologies drives the clustering mechanism. In that regard, Silicon Valley is exceptional, for it rests heavily on one technology—the semiconductor. When that technology and its products experienced little growth and went through a critical industrial phase in the early 1980s, Silicon Valley was hit hard. The Boston area high-technology cluster rests on a more diverse technology base, as does the Los Angeles area, the premier high-technology region in the United States.

But it takes more than technological inputs to feed the agglomeration effects described above. Venture capitalists, with their "smart" money, play a critical role in the high-risk, high-reward, high-technology industries. Social support for technology and for economic development is also critical to nurturing the proper institutional environment in which high-technology industries will thrive.

Growing a High-Technology Cluster

Many communities and states have been attempting to recreate Silicon Valley and Route 128 in their regions. A large number of clusters of high-technology firms already exist in the United States, Canada, Western Europe, and Japan. As mentioned earlier, the largest one in the United States is in Los Angeles. Southeast of Los Angeles, mainly in Orange County, lies the largest agglomeration of high-technology firms in the world. There are also several large high-technology clusters in the greater–New York area and Chicago areas.

Most of these high-technology clusters appeared without specific planning by state or local authorities. In fact, the artificially grown clusters are quite small and not that successful. The Research Triangle Park in North Carolina is world famous, but it provides only about 25,000 jobs, in about twenty-five or so organizations. The two largest employers, Northern Telecom and IBM, account for 15,000 jobs, and six other large organizations account for another 8,000. Smaller organizations account for the rest. On all counts, the Research Triangle Park is an artificial cluster. It does not have much internal dynamism and grows mostly by the addition of outside elements. The Park was started some thirty years ago, and even today, it remains a very expensive experiment.

The other planned clusters are much smaller. A few thousand jobs, usually around a university park, are the best that was achieved. Yet the failures of planned high-technology clusters do not do justice to many state and community interventions. While not as grandiose as the planning for a whole new industrial sector in a region, many individual policies contributed to the accelerated development of high-technology clusters.

Nurturing the growth of a cluster is a task that is slowly mastered. Many actions taken by communities and governments over the years now appear to be more effective than quick-fix solutions. On the other hand, many policies and measures have been proven ineffective. What works and what does not work is gradually being sorted out.

Most high-technology firms or establishments are run by entrepreneurs. They are new, small, dynamic firms that grow rapidly into medium-size and "fast-track" firms. New firms that grow from small to medium to large in less than one generation are under the leadership of entrepreneurs.

A high-technology cluster can be compared to a forest. The trees, plants, and bushes represent businesses of all sizes and shapes. One usually typifies a forest by its dominant species of trees, for example, a maple forest or a pine forest. Similarly, the economy of a region is often characterized by the traditional or high-technology sectors of its large firms. However, a detailed analysis would reveal that a considerable part of a forest's biomass consists of plants, bushes, sprouts, and small trees. Big trees are mature. From a growth perspective, they add little from year to year to the biomass. In fact, the disappearance of the old trees would contribute to a slow decline of the biomass if younger trees did not take their place. Growth occurs principally through a limited number of young sprouts. By analogy, young trees represent the fast-track firms, the dynamic, small businesses and new firms. Not all small plants contribute to growth because some die.

2
The Geography of High Technology

The success of Route 128, Silicon Valley, and a few high-technology parks, like the University City Science Center in Philadelphia and Stanford Research Park in Palo Alto, gives the impression that high technology is concentrated in a few select areas. This is not the case. High-technology industries are widely spread across North America. Silicon Valley, for instance, comprises less than 10 percent of high-technology employment in the United States and is not even the number one high-technology area. The Los Angeles–Long Beach area is the leading area, followed by the metropolitan New York area. Silicon Valley and Boston fall in third and fourth place, respectively.

Certain factors—major research universities, venture capital, urban amenities, and federal research and procurement policies—favor the concentration of high-technology industries in certain areas. But as clusters emerge, several other factors—the diffusion of knowledge through university research and training, widespread dispersion of entrepreneurship, the presence of numerous local markets served by locally based firms, and public policies to build regional infrastructures—tend to disperse high-technology activities. The influence of factors leading to a wide dissemination overshadows factors favoring concentration.

This chapter develops two points. First, although geographic clusters form during the early phases of developing high-technology industries, the diffusion process and the goal of serving metropolitan markets rapidly lead to the emergence and development of high-technology clusters in other metropolitan agglomerations. Second, focusing on well-known high-technology clusters, such as Silicon Valley, Route 128, or the Research Triangle, masks the fact that almost every metropolitan agglomeration has unique and diversified high-technology resources on which development strategies can be articulated.

The data on high-technology clusters in the United States, Canada, and Western Europe contradict the idea that high technology is concentrated in a few areas. In reality, high-technology firms, employment, and sectors are widely spread out in a large number of metropolitan agglomerations. High-technology activities are more widespread than is normally believed even although some concentrations around defense and aerospace sectors are evident.

A definition of high technology is needed as prior to looking at the data is a discussion of the importance of high technology in a modern economy.

Definition of the High-Technology Sector in an Industrial Economy

High technologies are scientific fields that find industrial applications to meet particular market needs. Thus, every period in history has its own particular set of high-technology industries. Textile machines, steam locomotives, machine tools, and electricity generation were once high-technology sectors. Today, biotechnology, biomedical instruments, semiconductors, information systems, computers, and software applications (especially in manufacturing) are considered high technology. Tomorrow's high technology sectors will certainly be different.

No consensus exists on the definition of the high-technology sector of the economy. To some, the term refers to industries involved with computers, telecommunications, electronics, and biotechnology. To others, high-technology industries are those emerging sectors experiencing rapid or radical technological changes. Many technologies perceived as advanced ten years ago have matured and are now considered standard. Such dynamism constantly changes the definition of the high-technology sector of the economy.

Three approaches can be used to identify the high-technology sector. None of them is totally satisfactory. One approach is to identify industries characterized by high research and development (R&D) intensity, that is, those sectors in which organized research is intensively pursued. Unfortunately, this approach, based on (R&D) efforts, is incomplete. For instance, it does not take into account newly created spin-offs that emerge on the basis of R&D performed elsewhere. Moreover, it is biased toward certain industrial sectors. The industry doing the most R&D in the United States, in absolute terms, is automobile design and assembly. General Motors always leads the annual lists of corporations with the largest R&D expenditures. The R&D criterion could also be applied to technology-based firms that allocate a substantial proportion of revenues to R&D. But again, certain sectors are discriminated against. In particular, this criterion usually short-changes service industries, because they spend little on R&D, or because R&D is embedded in the normal course of their activities.

A second approach is to identify all industries in which the proportion of engineers, scientists, and technicians to the total work force is high. This approach leads to the inclusion of mature manufacturing and service industries, which are not usually associated with leading-edge technologies. For instance, consulting engineering firms associated with road construction, bridges, etc., are ipso facto included in the high-technology sector. Manufacturing firms in traditional sectors such as textiles and railroad or metallic construction, which are experiencing high-productivity growth because they incorporate new technologies in their early process of diffusion, tend to be excluded.

A third approach uses scientific novelty as its criterion. This definition of the high-technology sector is too contingent upon present and fashionable scientific fields. Moreover, there is no objective base to determine scientific novelty. Patent registration and scientific publications are not always reliable indicators.

Thus, there is no single method to satisfactorily define high technology. Most researchers who have tackled this issue select a certain number of SIC codes and the industries they refer to, on the basis of prespecified criteria. We believe that the high-technology sector of the economy is best defined by those manufacturing or science industries in which the vast majority of firms spend a substantial proportion of sales revenues on R&D and employ a high proportion of scientists, engineers, and technicians. This approach permits the identification of industries that operate at the frontiers of knowledge and in sectors in which products and services have a high value-added content through the application of technology.

R&D Intensity

R&D intensity is the proportion of sales revenues invested in research and development activities. This criterion is affected by the age of the firm, and it should be adjusted accordingly. During the pre-start-up, or start-up, phase of a high-technology company, a large proportion of expenditures falls into the category of product development, even though such expenditures may not be accounted for as such. As sales rise, the proportion of revenue that is allocated to R&D falls. However, it can rise again, under the double effect of competitive pressures for new product architectures and the perceived potential fruitfulness of the technical fields in which the firm operates.

Employment of Scientists, Engineers, and Technicians

High-technology firms require highly qualified scientific staff to test, develop, and introduce innovative products and incorporate novel processes into their production systems through systematic use of scientific and technical knowledge. High-technology firms are engaged in the introduction of innovations, in the creative imitation of innovations introduced by pioneers, and in the early adoption of innovations in the process of diffusion. These intellectual and production tasks demand specialized personnel.

In operational terms, these two criterion must be translated into statistical parameters. Various operational definitions of high technology have been provided along these lines, in particular: the Bureau of Labor Statistics, the Office of Technology Assessment, the Brookings Institute, the Institute of Urban and Regional Studies at the University of California, and many state agencies that gather labor statistics.

Depending on the particular parameters used, the number of industries corresponding to three-digit SIC codes ranges from a minimum of six (Bureau of Labor Statistics) to thirty-nine (Office of Science and Technology). Some definitions include services and research institutions. Others exclude chemicals, metal working, and the communications industry. In Minnesota, for instance, thirty-six industries, defined by three-digit SIC codes, were selected to represent the high-technology sector of the economy. Such industries have a relatively high level of scientific, engineering, and technical workers, and a higher than average level of research and development spending.

We use a definition put forth by Robert Vinson that was adopted by the Commonwealth of Massachusetts. For statistical purposes, the high-technology sector is made of nineteen manufacturing and service industries, identified with a three-digit SIC code. Three additional SIC codes were added: ordnance and accessories, research and development organizations, and universities. These three additional fields are composed of organizations in which scientific and technical personnel is crucial. In particular, ordnance and accessories, a field characterized by large defense contracts, was added since most of the work done is performed by engineers and other highly skilled scientists on projects that often require leading-edge technologies. Table 2–1 lists the industries and SIC codes that form our operational definition of the high-technology sector of the economy.

This definition is not perfect. On one hand, some firms classified with these SIC codes are not necessarily high-technology companies. On the other hand, the subtle dynamics of emerging scientific sectors are also extremely difficult to capture with SIC codes. Whatever the definition, there are bound to be gray areas. Some industries make use of advanced-process technology but are excluded because their products are more typically associated with classical production methods. Some high-technology industries, such as electronics and inorganic chemicals, include certain firms that are little more than traditional manufacturing establishments. The same applies to computer and data processing services and engineering and architectural services. A broader-base definition seems more appropriate than a highly focused one. High technology loses some of its meaning when it is reduced to a few technological fields.

Table 2–1
Industries Classified as Part of the
High-Technology Sector

SIC Code	Industry
281	Industrial inorganic chemicals
282	Plastic materials and synthetics
283	Drugs
348	Ordinance and accessories
351	Engines and turbines
357	Office computing machinery
361	Electric distributing equipment
362	Electric industrial apparatus
366	Communications equipment
367	Electronic components and accessories
372	Aircraft and parts
376	Guided missiles, space vehicles, and parts
381	Engineering and scientific instruments
382	Measuring and controlling devices
383	Optical instruments and lenses
384	Medical instruments and supplies
386	Photographic equipment and supplies
737	Computer and data processing services
7391	Research and development labs
822	Universities
891	Engineering and architectural services
892	Noncommercial research organizations

The Importance of the High-Technology Sector in the Economy

How valuable is the high-technology sector to an economy? Employment and contribution to the growth of employment are usually used as the two main criteria. If employment is used as a criterion, one finds that the high-technology sector of the economy is characterized by the dominant presence of a limited number of large multiestablishment firms where much of the employment is concentrated. This suggests that a limited number of large firms provide the majority of high-technology jobs. However, most high-technology firms are small and grow at a faster rate than larger firms do. From a growth perspective, smaller firms are more valuable. They are the ones that are adding high-technology jobs to the economy.

Here are the main characteristics of the high-technology sector and its importance, based on the rather broad definition of high technology which we used.

Less than 2 percent of business establishments in the United States fall under the heading of high technology. They represent 7.4 percent of private sector employment. In manufacturing and business services, approximately 11 percent of business establishments and 21 percent of employment are in high technology.

The average number of employees in high-technology establishments is sixty-nine, twice that of the low-technology manufacturing sector, and five times the average in other industries dominated by the services sectors.

Large firms are more prominent in high technology than in other sectors of the economy. Almost 90 percent of employment in the high-technology sector is in firms with more than 100 employees. This, compares with 75 percent for the low-technology manufacturing and business service sector and 58 percent for all other industries. Yet, the high-technology sector is composed mostly of small and medium-sized firms. Employment is concentrated in a small fraction of large firms operating several branch plants. More than 50 percent of high-technology firms have fewer than twenty employees.

High-technology industries grow faster than the rest of the economy. They exhibit a high employment growth rate (4.5 percent) when compared to the overall economy (3.5 percent). High technology contributed approximately 10 percent of new net jobs between 1976 and 1980, most of them in large businesses.

High-technology employment broadly reflects the same spatial dispersion as overall employment between states and among the various metropolitan areas. The top ten states account for about 60 percent of high-technology employment and about 68 percent of total employment.

The formation of new business establishments is approximately 50 percent higher in high-technology sectors than for low-technology industries. Moreover, high-technology industries have higher growth rates than low-technology sectors. However, they are not necessarily the fast-growing industries. As a rule, new business formation and expansion rates in high technology are generally higher than for low-technology industries. Their closure and contraction rates are similar.

Multiunit firms are more prominent in high technology than in the other sectors of the economy. Single-establishment firms represent close to 60 percent of all high-technology establishments. But high-technology employment tends to be concentrated in multiestablishment firms. Only 12 percent of high-technology employment is in independent firms, while the rest is in branches or affiliates of local and national firms, or in firms with multiple establishments.

Single-establishment firms are multiplying faster than multi-establishment firms. They account for 54 percent of new establishments. Yet, the role of independent firms is less important in the high-technology sector than in the low-technology or service sector where they account for 70 percent of new establishments. Significant growth in the high-technology sectors occurs through the opening of branches and branch plants.

Although statistically, high-technology entrepreneurship through small firms is overwhelmed by large scale firms, it would be a mistake to discount the role that small firms play. One is well advised to recall the forest example used earlier. Large firms are the prominent old trees but the future of the forest is assured by the multitude of young saplings that may not be easily noticed by the casual observer.

Where Are the High-Technology Industries?

High technology is spread around the nation. But the extent of the dispersion varies significantly according to whether one looks at R&D expenditures, start-ups financed by venture capitalists, or at the firms that fall into the industrial categories defined as the high-technology sector of the economy. In order to capture the phenomenon of dispersion, we can look at high technology at three phases of an industry development. What one finds is that the dispersion varies according to the industry phase of development. Basic research expenditures are associated with the pre-start-up phase. Venture capital financing reflects the early stage of the development of a firm. Data on high-technology establishments and employment reflect an industry's maturity phase, as establishments multiply to fill every nook and cranny offered by the market place. The combination of these three cross-sections reveals the diffusion pattern of high technology, which leads to its observed dispersion.

A high degree of concentration exists for the R&D activities that precede the first "taste of market" for leading-edge technologies. Venture-capital financing is also concentrated, although less than basic research activities. By contrast, a wide dispersion of high-technology firms and industries into numerous metropolitan agglomerations is evident.

Table 2–2
High-Technology Clusters, 1984

	High-Technology	
Cluster	*Establishments*	*Employment*
1. Los Angeles	7,919	519,305
2. Metropolitan New York and New Jersey	7,415	360,917
3. Silicon Valley	4,133	309,416
4. Route 128	2,602	254,557
5. Chicago	3,303	208,891
6. Delaware Valley	1,716	151,607
7. Dallas/Forth Worth	2,113	132,752
8. Baltimore/Washington	2,565	118,226
9. Austin	2,082	114,820
10. Buffalo/Rochester	679	114,033
11. New Haven/Stamford	1,242	97,405
12. San Diego	1,511	77,144
13. Seattle	1,281	73,593
14. Houston	2,413	71,840
15. Minneapolis/St. Paul	1,176	70,223
16. Denver/Boulder	1,140	64,411
17. Phoenix	1,086	63,888
18. St. Louis	600	57,031
19. Raleigh/Durham	565	53,718
20. Detroit	1,513	48,077
21. Salt Lake City	570	45,239
22. Pittsburgh	693	42,940
23. Milwaukee	555	42,451
24. Portland, Oregon	673	38,309
25. Atlanta	918	32,314
26. Tampa	797	27,374
27. Kansas City	265	26,069
28. Santa Fe	351	18,749
29. Columbus	497	17,011
30. Lexington	153	11,807
Total	52,526	3,264,117

Dispersion of High-Technology Activities

The wide dispersion of high-technology activities into numerous metropolitan sectors in the United States is illustrated in table 2–2, which gives the distribution of firms and employment in thirty metropolitan agglomerations.

The thirty metropolitan areas that serve to identify high technology clusters are defined in the appendix. Each cluster is characterized by one or more of the following criteria: the presence of high-technology firms, growing high-technology employment, a strong industrial base on which high technology can grow, and the presence of research universities or government laboratories. The data was drawn from the County Business Patterns published by the U.S. Census Bureau.

High-technology activities are spread around. The Los Angeles and the New York areas, (the latter includes the Newark area but excludes Stamford and New Haven) host the two largest clusters, followed by Silicon Valley, Route 128, and Chicago. These five metropolitan areas represent over half of the total employment among the thirty clusters and nearly half the establishments. As a matter of fact, the metropolitan Los Angeles, New York, and Chicago areas, not particularly known for high-technology activities, represent close to 30 percent of firms and 30 percent of employment of the high-technology sector. Well-known areas such as Route 128 and Silicon Valley account for smaller proportions than these three metropolitan agglomerations.

In 1984, twenty metropolitan agglomerations in our survey had more than 1,000 high-technology firms or more than 50,000 persons employed in high technology. Even areas with mature industries such as Detroit, Philadelphia, and Pittsburgh housed substantial high-technology clusters.

Growth of High-Technology Establishments. The annual increase in high-technology establishments, which includes both independent businesses and branch plants, has been substantial from 1971 to 1984, as indicated by table 2–3. In Los Angeles, the annual increase in establishments has been close to 300, while Route 128 added approximately 100 new establishments per year.

The growth of high-technology establishments from 1971 to 1984 has been exceptionally high in Los Angeles (4,122) and metropolitan New York and New Jersey (2,926), ahead of Silicon Valley (2,882) or Route 128 (1,270). Most regions, especially the larger ones such as Los Angeles, Route 128 and New York–New Jersey, experienced annual rates of growth of new high-technology establishments below 10 percent. Metropolitan areas that have experienced exceptionally high annual rates of growth over 20 percent are Seattle, San Diego, Phoenix, Tampa, and Houston. Silicon Valley, Austin, Baltimore-Washington, Salt Lake City, Dallas, St. Louis, and Denver experienced growth rates of between 15 and 20 percent in the 1971–84 period.

Growth in High-Technology Employment. In terms of high-technology employment, our data indicate that many regional agglomerations have grown faster than others. Table 2–4 shows that in thirteen regional agglomerations high-technology employment grew at an annual rate greater than 10 percent. The fast growing high-technology agglomerations in terms of employment include Seattle, San Diego, Phoenix, Florida, Texas, Silicon Valley, and the Research Triangle. Amongst the slow growing high-technology metropolitan agglomerations were New York, Delaware Valley, Route 128, Detroit, and Chicago.

Table 2–3
Growth in High-Technology Establishments, 1971–1984

Cluster	Rank by Additional High-Technology Establishments	Additional High-Technology Establishments	Annual Rate of Growth
Los Angeles	1	4,122	9.05%
Metropolitan New York and New Jersey	2	2,926	5.20
Silicon Valley	3	2,882	19.20
Baltimore/Washington	4	1,758	18.15
Houston	5	1,741	21.59
Austin	6	1,434	18.44
Dallas	7	1,415	16.89
Chicago	8	1,368	5.89
Route 128	9	1,270	7.95
Seattle	10	1,186	104.00
San Diego	11	1,160	27.54
Phoenix	12	803	23.65
Denver/Boulder	13	744	15.66
Detroit	14	688	6.95
Minneapolis/St. Paul	15	661	10.70
New Haven/Stamford	16	631	8.61
Delaware Valley	17	586	4.32
Tampa	18	581	22.42
Atlanta	19	560	13.04
Portland, Oregon	20	418	13.66
St. Louis	21	399	16.54
Salt Lake City	22	385	17.34
Raleigh/Durham	23	359	14.52
Pittsburgh	24	285	5.82
Buffalo/Rochester	25	260	5.17
Columbus	26	248	8.30
Santa Fe	27	197	10.66
Lexington	28	79	8.90
Milwaukee	29	73	1.26
Kansas City	30	54	2.13

Table 2–4
Growth in High-Technology Employment, 1971–1984

Cluster	Rank by Additional High-Technology Employment	Additional High-Technology Employment	Annual Rate of Growth
Los Angeles	1	238,395	38.98%
Silicon Valley	2	221,614	33.31
Route 128	3	139,209	28.25
Metropolitan New York and New Jersey	4	67,172	23.04
Baltimore/Washington	5	65,299	20.76
San Diego	6	63,557	16.49
Denver/Boulder	7	51,522	15.88
Dallas	8	46,937	14.40
Austin	9	45,832	12.26
Houston	10	42,506	12.08
Delaware Valley	11	41,013	11.27
St. Louis	12	40,694	10.28
New Haven/Stamford	13	39,972	10.06
Phoenix	14	36,734	7.80
Seattle	15	35,569	7.07
Raleigh/Durham	16	34,028	7.06
Buffalo/Rochester	17	32,520	5.80
Salt Lake City	18	30,054	5.54
Portland, Oregon	19	29,582	4.64
Milwaukee	20	27,840	4.56
Chicago	21	25,422	3.47
Minneapolis/St. Paul	22	25,124	3.32
Atlanta	23	22,184	3.09
Tampa	24	20,102	2.88
Kansas City	25	15,520	2.80
Pittsburgh	26	12,634	1.85
Santa Fe	27	12,570	1.85
Detroit	28	8,730	1.83
Lexington	29	5,414	1.15
Columbus	30	− 2,602	− 1.11

High-Technology Density. The importance of high technology in the various regional economies varies greatly. This is what density measures. Worthy of note is the fact that the importance of high-technology activities amongst industrial and commercial activities is low even in the most well-known clusters. Nowhere do high-technology firms represent more than 4 percent of all establishments, as indicated in table 2–5. For employment the percentage is somewhat higher, but still relatively low.

Silicon Valley and Route 128, two well-known high-technology agglomerations rank first and second in terms of high-technology density with approximately 20 percent of employment and 4 percent of establishments falling into the high-technology category.

Employment density and establishment density are not perfectly correlated. In some metropolitan regions, the presence of small high-technology establishments appears to be more important while in others, larger establishments seem more prevalent. Table 2–6 shows the distribution of areas according to employment establishment. Two groups can be defined. The first group is characterized by higher levels of entrepreneurial activities, and in the second, high-technology establishments tend to be large manufacturing facilities or affiliates.

The first group is represented by Minneapolis/St. Paul, Denver, Baltimore/Washington, Austin, Dallas, and Houston and is characterized by a higher density of smaller establishments. The second group, represented by Kansas City, Route 128, Raleigh/Durham, Buffalo/Rochester, St. Louis, and Lexington, is characterized by the presence of large establishments.

Diversity of the Technology Base. High-technology agglomerations are usually known for strengths in particular technical fields. Thus, Boston is known for electronics and minicomputers, Los Angeles for defense and aerospace, and Minneapolis/St. Paul for supercomputers. To assess the degree of diversity in each metropolitan area, we have measured the number of establishments and the employment levels for ten broadly determined technical sectors: electronic components and instruments, defense and aerospace, pharmaceuticals and chemicals, data processing services, advanced manufacturing technologies, communications, biomedical instruments, computers, university research, and R&D and professional services.

Table 2–7 gives the ranking of number of establishments for the ten technical sectors. The dominant positions of Los Angeles, Silicon Valley, metropolitan New York–New Jersey, Massachusetts, and even Chicago in almost each of the technical areas are worthy of mention. Large high-technology agglomerations tend to be strong in each of the technical fields. Indeed, most areas show strengths in more than one field.

An index of diversity has been built to capture the degree to which the

Table 2–5
Density of High Technology in Metropolitan Agglomerations, 1984

Cluster	Density of High Technology among Establishments	Density of High Technology in Employment
1. Silicon Valley	4.43%	21.97%
2. Route 128	3.96	19.98
3. Baltimore/Washington	3.52	10.28
4. Houston	3.37	5.92
5. San Diego	3.31	14.07
6. Denver	3.29	12.41
7. Seattle	3.17	13.12
8. Austin	3.11	10.08
9. Minneapolis/St. Paul	3.02	9.26
10. Los Angeles	2.98	12.87
11. Connecticut	2.96	15.26
12. Dallas	2.73	9.97
13. Santa Fe	2.67	11.80
14. Atlanta	2.64	5.27
15. Arizona	2.63	11.40
16. Kentucky	2.52	13.34
17. Metropolitan New York and New Jersey	2.49	6.62
18. Salt Lake City	2.49	14.26
19. St. Louis	2.45	13.73
20. Research Triangle Park	2.43	14.09
21. Columbus	2.43	4.89
22. Chicago	2.38	8.35
23. Portland, Oregon	2.25	9.81
24. Pittsburgh	2.22	8.02
25. Delaware Valley	2.17	11.19
26. Detroit	2.16	4.24
27. Tampa	2.09	5.62
28. Buffalo/Rochester	1.97	19.40
29. Milwaukee	1.90	8.47
30. Kansas City	1.63	9.00

ten technical areas are actively represented in each regional agglomeration. Table 2–8 gives an ordering from the most diverse to the least diverse regional high-technology clusters in terms of the distribution of employment across the ten technical sectors. Most agglomerations show a high degree of diversity across technical sectors. Moreover, a reasonably parallel association seems to exist between the size of the agglomeration and its degree of technical diversity.

Metropolitan New York–New Jersey, Chicago, New Haven/Stamford, Silicon Valley, and the Twin Cities score high in the diversity of employment. Route 128 scores high in the diversity of establishments across the ten technical fields. Only a few clusters are highly concentrated in selected technical sectors such as Kentucky in communications, computers, and R&D and

Table 2–6
High-Technology Employment per
Establishment, 1984

Cluster	Average Number of Employees per High-Technology Establishment
1. Buffalo/Rochester	167.94
2. Kansas City	98.37
3. Route 128	97.83
4. Raleigh/Durham	95.08
5. St. Louis	95.05
6. Delaware Valley	88.35
7. Salt Lake City	79.37
8. New Haven/Stamford	78.43
9. Lexington	77.17
10. Milwaukee	76.49
11. Silicon Valley	74.86
12. Los Angeles	65.58
13. Chicago	63.24
14. Dallas	62.83
15. Pittsburgh	61.96
16. Minneapolis/St. Paul	59.71
17. Phoenix	58.83
18. Seattle	57.45
19. Portland, Oregon	56.92
20. Denver/Boulder	56.50
21. Austin	55.15
22. Santa Fe	53.42
23. San Diego	51.05
24. Metropolitan New York and New Jersey	48.67
25. Baltimore/Washington	46.09
26. Atlanta	35.20
27. Tampa	34.35
28. Columbus	34.23
29. Detroit	31.78
30. Houston	29.77

professional services, or New Mexico in defense and aerospace, communications, and R&D and professional services.

Growth rates differ among technology sectors. Some technical sectors had extremely high growth rates, such as data processing services that went from a few firms mostly in Silicon Valley to a huge number of widely distributed firms. Most sectors experienced growth patterns that led roughly to a doubling of the number of establishments from 1971 to 1984. Only two sectors experienced a net contraction in the number of firms: defense and aerospace, and pharmaceuticals, chemicals, and drugs. Table 2–9 gives the growth of establishments and employment for each of the ten technical sectors.

Canada

Canada has high-technology clusters in Toronto, Montreal, and Ottawa. These three high-technology clusters are comparable to mid-size clusters in the United States. Table 2–10 shows the number of high-technology firms in Toronto, Montreal, and Ottawa.

The two large metropolitan agglomerations of Toronto and Montreal exhibit strengths in a number of technical fields such as defense and aerospace, pharmaceuticals, communications, electronics, and advanced manufacturing techniques. Press reports in Canada have stressed the role of the Ottawa metropolitan region by calling it a Silicon Valley of the North. In fact, electronics and telecommunications are important sectors for Ottawa, but this cluster is much smaller in size than the two large metropolitan agglomerations of Toronto and Montreal.

Western Europe

High-technology clusters exist in many regions of Western Europe. However, comparable statistical data on the high-technology activities in the different regions and countries do not exist. The evidence available is less formalized and varies from country to country. Here is a short description of the best-known clusters.

West London. The West London high-technology cluster is probably the largest one in Western Europe. About two thousand high-technology firms in electronics, computing, software, and data processing are located around the M-3 and M-4 motorways west of Heathrow Airport. This high-technology cluster grew through independent start-ups and spin-offs from large American high-technology firms with European headquarters and from British technology-based firms.

Cambridge. The Cambridge high-technology cluster, fifty miles east of London, is smaller but highly diversified. It grew around the industrial park established near the university and the new towns. The Cambridge phenomenon of start-ups and technology-based firms has been a fertile field for the British venture capital industry for some time. A recent study counted 261 firms, 75 percent of which are independent local firms, and 25 percent branches or subsidiaries. The net rate of business creation has been around fifteen per year. Table 2–11 shows the sectorial distribution of companies in the Cambridge area.

South Wales. The South Wales cluster is essentially a series of branch plants, with approximately 20,000 technology jobs. Japanese, British, and American

Table 2–7
High-Technology Establishments in Ten Technical Fields, 1984

	Electronic Components & Instruments		Data Processing		Communications
Los Angeles	800	Metro New York and New Jersey	2,272	Los Angeles	520
Silicon Valley	546			Metro New York and New Jersey	442
Metro New York and New Jersey	544	Los Angeles	1,728		
		Chicago	960	Silicon Valley	257
Chicago	274	Silicon Valley	950	Chicago	240
Massachusetts	204	Maryland	802	Massachusetts	141
Dallas	126	Massachusetts	681	Dallas	109
Connecticut	125	Dallas	623	California	103
California	120	Austin	618	Connecticut	102
Austin	119	Houston	556	Austin	102
Philadelphia	101	Philadelphia	436	Michigan	91
Arizona	81	Michigan	390	Houston	90
Minnesota	80	Minnesota	327	Philadelphia	85
Michigan	66	Connecticut	316	Maryland	75
Buffalo/Rochester	57	Georgia	290	Milwaukee	65
Seattle	54	Seattle	286	Minnesota	63
Maryland	49	California	271	Washington	60
Houston	49	Colorado	254	Buffalo/Rochester	50
Colorado	45	Arizona	223	Arizona	43
Oregon	41	St. Louis	177	Florida	36
Florida	38	Oregon	162	Pittsburgh	35
Milwaukee	35	Buffalo/Rochester	150	St. Louis	27
Utah	27	Florida	149	Colorado	26
North Carolina	25	Pittsburgh	149	Georgia	24
Pittsburgh	18	North Carolina	140	Oregon	23
Columbus	18	Milwaukee	132	North Carolina	22
New Mexico	17	Utah	127	Columbus	20
St. Louis	17	Columbus	123	Utah	19
Georgia	15	Kansas City	76	New Mexico	7
Kansas City	9	New Mexico	64	Kansas City	5
Kentucky	5	Kentucky	24	Kentucky	1
	3,705		13,456		2,883

	Manufacturing Technologies		*Universities*		*Defense & Aerospace*
Los Angeles	288	Metro New York and New Jersey	216	Los Angeles	394
Metro New York and New Jersey	263	Los Angeles	130	Metro New York and New Jersey	103
Silicon Valley	231	Chicago	97	Seattle	60
Massachusetts	142	Philadelphia	79	Dallas	50
Chicago	119	Massachusetts	63	Connecticut	26
Philadelphia	82	Maryland	56	Phoenix	35
Michigan	76	Silicon Valley	48	California	35
Connecticut	76	Georgia	35	Detroit	34
Houston	75	Michigan	33	Chicago	24
California	66	Austin	31	Austin	24
Maryland	55	Dallas	30	Silicon Valley	18
Austin	43	Buffalo/Rochester	30	Milwaukee	18
Dallas	41	Minnesota	28	Houston	17
Minnesota	34	California	26	Philadelphia	16
Washington	29	St. Louis	23	Minnesota	14
Colorado	28	Arizona	22	Utah	10
Arizona	26	Pittsburgh	21	St. Louis	10
Buffalo/Rochester	24	Houston	20	Buffalo/Rochester	8
Milwaukee	24	Milwaukee	17	Massachusetts	8
Oregon	21	Colorado	16	Florida	7
Pittsburgh	15	Connecticut	16	Oregon	6
Florida	14	Kansas City	16	Kansas City	5
Columbus	14	Oregon	14	Maryland	4
North Carolina	10	Washington	14	Georgia	4
St. Louis	9	Columbus	14	Colorado	3
Kansas City	7	North Carolina	12	New Mexico	2
New Mexico	7	Florida	11	Columbus	2
Utah	5	Kentucky	6	Pittsburgh	2
Georgia	4	New Mexico	6	North Carolina	1
Kentucky	0	Utah	4	Kentucky	0
	1,828		1,134		950

Table 2–7 continued

	Biomedical & Optical Instruments		R&D & Professional Services		Pharmaceuticals and Chemicals
Los Angeles	336	Los Angeles	3,188	Metro New York and New Jersey	313
Metro New York and New Jersey	279	Metro New York and New Jersey	2,862	Los Angeles	232
Chicago	139	Silicon Valley	1,523	Silicon Valley	86
Silicon Valley	130	Houston	1,477	Chicago	76
Massachusetts	117	Maryland	1,451	Houston	73
Philadelphia	80	Chicago	1,314	Philadelphia	61
California	62	Massachusetts	1,064	Massachusetts	49
Minnesota	61	Austin	1,013	Dallas	46
Connecticut	60	Dallas	991	Austin	40
Dallas	44	California	762	Connecticut	31
Buffalo/Rochester	43	Philadelphia	755	Michigan	31
Colorado	37	Michigan	733	Buffalo/Rochester	25
Washington	36	Washington	699	Pittsburgh	24
Austin	35	Colorado	698	Georgia	24
Houston	31	Arizona	596	Utah	22
Oregon	30	Georgia	503	Arizona	21
Florida	28	Florida	495	North Carolina	20
Utah	28	Minnesota	494	St. Louis	18
Michigan	26	Connecticut	450	Columbus	18
Maryland	25	Pittsburgh	399	California	17
St. Louis	22	Oregon	342	Milwaukee	16
Pittsburgh	21	North Carolina	319	Minnesota	16
Milwaukee	13	Utah	301	Colorado	14
Arizona	13	St. Louis	283	Oregon	13
Columbus	13	Buffalo/Rochester	273	Florida	12
Kansas City	10	Columbus	263	Maryland	11
Georgia	9	New Mexico	239	Washington	8
New Mexico	5	Milwaukee	235	Kansas City	6
North Carolina	2	Kansas City	131	Kentucky	3
Kentucky	0	Kentucky	112	New Mexico	0
	1,735		23,965		1,326

	Computers		Total High Technology Establishments
Silicon Valley	344	Los Angeles	7,919
Los Angeles	303	Metro New York and New Jersey	7,415
Massachusetts	133		
Metro New York and New Jersey	121	Silicon Valley	4,133
		Chicago	3,303
Chicago	60	Massachusetts	2,602
Minnesota	59	Maryland	2,565
Austin	57	Houston	2,413
Dallas	53	Dallas	2,113
California	49	Austin	2,082
Maryland	37	Philadelphia	1,716
Washington	35	Michigan	1,513
Michigan	33	California	1,511
Connecticut	30	Washington	1,281
Utah	27	Connecticut	1,242
Arizona	26	Minnesota	1,176
Houston	25	Colorado	1,140
Philadelphia	21	Arizona	1,086
Oregon	21	Georgia	918
Buffalo/Rochester	19	Florida	797
Colorado	19	Pittsburgh	693
St. Louis	14	Buffalo/Rochester	679
North Carolina	14	Oregon	673
Columbus	12	St. Louis	600
Georgia	10	Utah	570
Pittsburgh	9	North Carolina	565
Florida	7	Milwaukee	555
New Mexico	4	Columbus	497
Kentucky	1	New Mexico	351
Milwaukee	0	Kansas City	265
Kansas City	0	Kentucky	153
	1,544		52,526

Table 2–8
Technological Diversity for Each Cluster, 1984

Cluster	Ranking of High-Technology Diversity as Measured by Employment
Metropolitan New York and New Jersey	1
New Haven/Stamford	2
Chicago	2
Silicon Valley	4
Twin Cities	5
Detroit	5
San Diego	7
Austin	8
Los Angeles	8
Columbus	10
Route 128	11
Dallas/Fort Worth	12
Denver/Boulder	13
Delaware Valley	14
Pittsburgh	15
Phoenix	15
Kansas City	15
Salt Lake City	18
Raleigh/Durham	19
Houston	20
Milwaukee	21
Oregon	22
Baltimore/Washington	23
Tampa	24
Georgia	25
Buffalo/Rochester	26
Santa Fe	27
St. Louis	28
Seattle	29
Lexington	30

Table 2-9
Growth of High-Technology Sectors, 1971–1984

	Employment Growth				Establishment Growth			
	Total Employment		Net Change	Annual Growth Rate	Total Establishments		Net Change	Annual Growth Rate
	1971	1984			1971	1984		
Electronic components	241,782	380,782	139,000	3.6%	1,061	3,705	1,744	10.9%
Defense and aerospace	315,408	508,843	193,435	3.7	1,360	950	−410	−2.7
Pharmaceuticals	164,612	120,345	−44,267	−2.4	1,712	1,326	−386	−1.9
Data processing services	51,307	283,338	232,031	14.0	1,880	13,456	11,576	16.3
Advanced manufacturing technology	76,251	162,032	85,781	6.0	787	1,828	1,041	6.7
Communications	388,485	482,216	93,731	1.7	2,513	2,883	370	1.06
Biomedical and optical	49,070	102,495	53,425	5.8	985	1,735	750	4.5
Computers	123,739	269,300	145,561	6.2	600	1,544	944	8.2
University research	240,872	527,506	286,634	6.2	753	1,134	381	3.4
R&D centers and professional services	224,067	427,260	203,197	5.1	12,548	23,965	11,417	5.5

Table 2–10
Number of High-Technology Firms and Employees in Toronto, Montreal, and Ottawa, 1986

	Toronto	Montreal	Ottawa
High-technology manufacturing firms	569	450	131
Approximate number of high-technology service firms	700	650	200
High-technology manufacturing employees	59,287	41,711	11,950
Distribution of manufacturing firms by size			
1–19 employees	241	205	71
20–99 employees	179	154	39
100 or more employees	119	91	21

Table 2–11
High-Technology Firms in the Cambridge, England, Area, 1985

	Establishments	Employment	Turnover
Chemicals/biotechnology	4%	9%	15%
Electrical equipment	3	2	2
Electronics capital goods	22	21	14
Other electronics	10	11	16
Instrument engineering	17	22	14
Computer hardware	11	7	23
Computer software	23	8	8
Consultancy/R&D	6	17	7
Other	4	3	1
Total	100	100	100
Total absolute value	261	13,700	£890m

Source: Segal, Quince and Partners, 1985.

electronic firms have established manufacturing plants to serve the export market. Its primary attraction has been subsidies and proximity to the West London corridor.

Central Scotland. Central Scotland emerged as a high-technology cluster through spin-offs from Ferranti (a large electronics firm which moved R&D and manufacturing facilities there during World War II) and from branch plants established by American firms. This cluster covers a 100-mile zone from the southwest of Glasgow to the northeast of Edinburgh. It consists of more than 400 electronics branch plants of American and Japanese semiconductor firms and a small number of home-grown companies. This cluster is second in importance after West London. Originally based on investments by large firms only, the area has begun to emerge as a high-technology cluster in its own right. Subsidiaries have developed considerable autonomy in R&D, product development, and marketing. Manufacturers and suppliers employ more than 40,000 persons. The most important sectors are defense electronics, telecommunications, and components. New start-ups account for approximately 10 percent of establishments. The predominance of production activities distinguishes the Central Scotland cluster from the West London Corridor.

Torino. The region of Torino in Northern Italy houses a high-technology cluster that emerged as electronics, robotics, and computer firms were set up to supply established firms, mainly in the automobile industry. During the 1971 to 1981 period, the number of industrial establishments has risen by close to 50 percent in the provinces of Torino and Piedmont, with small firms (below twenty employees) accounting for 33 percent of employment. The emergence of this high-technology cluster is due to the procurement policies of large firms such as Fiat and Olivetti, which were themselves undergoing radical transformations. A large number of advanced manufacturing techniques, and computer and electronics firms were created by entrepreneurs or as joint ventures with established firms.

West Germany. West Germany has two major high-technology clusters around the Hamburg/Hanover and Munich/Nuremberg areas. The highest concentration of high-technology firms is found in Bavaria and Baden Wurtemberg in the Munich/Nuremberg axis. These high-technology clusters are based on defense and aerospace, pharmaceuticals, electronics, electrical machinery, and precision manufacturing. A number of smaller high-technology concentrations can also be found around Karlsruhe and Berlin.

Paris. The southern part of the Paris region houses over a thousand high-technology establishments, including corporate research centers and government laboratories. It is probably the largest concentration in France. Since the early 1960s, a large number of government laboratories and technical universities have moved to this area. However, few spin-offs have emerged and collaboration with established industries and universities has not been very fruitful.

Grenoble. The Grenoble area is the second largest agglomeration of high technology in France. It is based mostly on electronics, advanced manufacturing, computers, and government research laboratories. This area has approximately 300 high-technology firms. The high-technology cluster around Grenoble is not a fully spontaneous one: it is still heavily dependent on a large number of government-sponsored laboratories.

Geographic Concentration during the Early Stages of Development

If high-technology activities are dispersed in many metropolitan agglomerations around the world, concentrations do exist during the early stages of the birth of new industrial sectors. Let's look at R&D activities and venture-capital financing.

Industrial R&D

Industrial R&D tends to be concentrated close to corporate headquarters. Location decisions for R&D establishments lead not only to the selection of sites near headquarters, but also to the grouping of laboratories in specialized agglomerations. Centralized industrial R&D activities are usually located near headquarters in suburban areas or near key manufacturing plants. Decentralized R&D facilities tend to be close to production facilities where interactions between R&D, manufacturing, and marketing can be organized to enhance product development abilities.

The overall effect of disaggregated corporate R&D location decisions leads to a high degree of concentration of industrial R&D in a few urban areas that offer high-quality scientific employees. Federal government and university R&D activities that are not as concentrated in major urban centers as private laboratories contribute to a dispersion of R&D away from large urban areas.

Leading-Edge Technologies

To assess geographic concentration of innovative research in the very early phases of new technologies, we examined the distribution of awards for Small Business Innovation Research in the U.S. federal government. Small Business Innovation Research (SBIR) grants are used to fund high-risk, high-pay-off, front-end research that is expected to lead to start-ups based on radically new technologies.

The Small Business Innovation Research program aims at setting aside a proportion of U.S. federal expenditure for R&D for small and emerging high-technology firms that cannot benefit from R&D tax credits. Federal agencies of the U.S. government from the Department of Defense to the Nuclear Regulatory Commission must earmark over the years up to 1.25 percent of their research funds for small business.

SBIR funds are awarded to firms with less than 500 employees in a three stage process. First, government agencies develop research topics and publish solicitations. Winners from this phase (usually one out of eleven) receive $20,000–$30,000 for six months to demonstrate the technical feasibility of their proposals. Successful completion qualifies firms for product development awards ranging from $250,000 to $500,000 for a period of two years. Half of the qualified applicants receive product development funding. Once product development is well along and the product concept has aroused interest, it is expected that start-ups or expansions will occur as a result of contracts from private firms or government agencies.

A very high degree of concentration in SBIR grants is evident. States and metropolitan areas with a strong high-technology industrial and research base and with universities housing engineering and scientific centers of excellence obtain a high proportion of awards. Table 2–12 shows the number of proposals and awards by state in the first seven years of the SBIR program.

Even though SBIR grants are only one of the many indicators of the early phases of innovation activities based on cutting-edge technologies, a high degree of geographical concentration in California and Massachusetts is evident. When considering all Phase I SBIR awards, from all U.S. federal departments, the distribution is not much different than that which exists in National Science Foundation (NSF) funding. Table 2–13 displays the geographic distribution of all Phase I SBIR awards for the top fifteen states.

Venture Capital

The venture-capital industry, whether organized or informal, provides early stage developmental funding as well as expansion financing for small companies that have implemented a sound business strategy and do not yet have access to public stock offerings. Venture capitalists seek investment opportunities in niches that have high growth potential but are presently too small to attract entries by large technology-based firms.

A very high degree of geographic concentration of financing of new high-technology companies by the professionally organized venture-capital industry can be inferred from an analysis of table 2–14. This estimate has been derived by Venture Economics from an analysis of 1,283 venture-based high-technology companies in areas such as computers and information analysis, electronics, advanced materials, vehicles mechanics, energy conservation, environment, and life sciences. As table 2–14 indicates, formal venture-capital investment in high technology is even more highly concentrated in California, Massachusetts, and Texas than SBIR awards.

Table 2–12
Proposals and Awards for Phase I SBIR Funding by the National Science
Foundation, 1977–1984

	Proposals	*Awards*	*Success Rate*
Massachusetts	612	128	20.9%
California	977	104	10.6
Maryland	312	34	10.9
Utah	148	26	17.6
New York	293	24	8.2
Virginia	257	21	8.2
Pennsylvania	183	20	10.9
Ohio	181	17	9.4
New Jersey	183	17	9.3
Colorado	166	17	10.2
Washington	136	15	11.0
Texas	182	14	7.7
Michigan	105	12	11.4
Oregon	47	10	21.3
Connecticut	121	9	7.4
North Carolina	50	9	18.0
Minnesota	46	8	17.4
Florida	83	7	8.4
Illinois	122	7	5.7
West Virginia	46	6	13.0
Maine	25	5	20.0

Source: National Science Foundation, 1986.

Key Factors for Growth

The growth of high-technology clusters in the different metropolitan agglomerations is associated with, but not fully explained by, the general growth in employment and establishments in these metropolitan areas. In fact, the correlation coefficient between growth of high-technology establishments and the overall growth of establishments is low. Catherine Armington, of the Brookings Institute, has noted that the relationship between business formation in high technology and employment growth in metropolitan areas is weak. (In fact, the correlation of high-technology business formations with metropolitan employment growth was small and negative.) City size had a

**Table 2–13
Geographic Distribution of SBIR Phase I Awards
for Funding Year 1983**

Top 15 states	
California	21.6%
Massachusetts	16.8
Virginia	6.7
Maryland	5.1
Ohio	4.1
Washington	4.1
Texas	3.5
Pennsylvania	3.5
New York	3.1
Connecticut	2.8
Colorado	2.3
Alabama	2.2
North Carolina	2.2
New Jersey	2.0
Utah	1.7
Other states	18.3

Source: Venture Economics, 1985.

small but positive association with business formation rates in both the high and low-technology sectors. Although new business formation as a whole is roughly proportional to employment growth, the same is not observed in the case of high technology.

Thus, the growth of high-technology activities cannot be explained simply by the size or by the general growth of population or employment in a metropolitan area. A distinct explanation has to be given for the growth of high-technology clusters in different metropolitan areas. The key factors that contribute to the emergence of high-technology clusters follow.

Military expenditures for R&D and procurement have been proposed as a major factor affecting both high-technology and the location of defense and aerospace industries. This government-originated demand has been found to be the only variable that is statistically related, although in a weak fashion, to the distribution of high-technology activities.

Table 2–14
Geographic Distribution of Technology-Based
Firms Financed by Formal Venture Capital,
1982–1984

Top 12 states	
California	41.4%
Massachusetts	16.3
Texas	5.7
Colorado	3.7
New York	3.6
Minnesota	3.4
Connecticut	2.4
New Jersey	2.3
Oregon	2.3
Michigan	1.9
Illinois	1.9
Washington	1.8
Other states	13.3

Source: Venture Economics, 1985.

The industry life-cycle theory indicates that high-technology activities branch out into low-cost areas. In fact, high-technology employment is heavily concentrated in the large establishments of multiplant firms. The branching out process from highly innovative regions to areas where costs are lower is spreading high-technology activities to many regions and counties but not necessarily to all metropolitan areas equally.

Metropolitan agglomerations possess distinct or competitive advantages that can lead to the creation of high-technology firms. For instance, a city may house a number of teaching and clinical hospitals that are oriented towards leading-edge research in the biomedical field and from which a flow of small biomedical or biotechnology firms can emerge. A metropolitan area may have built over many generations the infrastructure of universities, advanced research laboratories, venture capital, and stimulating incubators that provide advantages to entrepreneurs.

In large metropolitan areas, market opportunities are provided to technical entrepreneurs by manufacturing and commercial firms. For example, numerous advanced manufacturing technologies firms are created to provide services to regional manufacturers. In the same fashion, software companies are established to provide information systems services to stock brokers, banks, trusts, and manufacturing companies that thrive in metropolitan agglomerations.

The diffusion of scientific and technical knowledge on which high-technology start-ups are based occurs through university research and teaching. The movement of faculty members and the training of graduate students are means by which this information flows. Organized technology transfers from government laboratories, university or advanced laboratories can lead to emergence of new activities. Technology can also be transferred by spin-offs, recruitment of personnel, purchase of equipment, and licenses.

Part II
The Emergence of Regional High-Technology Clusters

The nurturing of high-technology firms and industries is of vital importance for the rejuvenation of the economic structure of any nation or region. Without a replenishing of the stock of firms by start-ups or corporate ventures to compensate for closures and contractions, the regional industrial base ages, and the ability to compete dwindles. The presence of large profitable technology-based firms in a region can maintain the appearance of regional prosperity. However, this temporary illusion of prosperity can also hide the fact that the next generations of firms in emerging industries are not being developed.

The purpose of part II is to illustrate with a model the process of emergence of self-sustaining high-technology clusters. Chapter 3 sketches our conceptual model and outlines avenues for the growth of high-technology activities in a region and the types of clusters that may arise. Chapter 4 describes the processes that support entrepreneurial actions and eventually lead to agglomeration effects. Chapter 5 depicts the technical, social, and business inputs of the infrastructure that buttresses these processes.

3
An Institutional Approach to the Emergence of High-Technology Clusters

etermining the causes behind the emergence of high-technology clusters is not an easy task, as econometricians have discovered. Attempts to identify clear causal factors that could suggest policy initiatives have pointed to the influence of many variables, but few are consistently and statistically significant. Military spending, the presence of research-intensive universities, and labor-force composition appear as significant variables, but they explain only a small part of the phenomenon.

Econometric studies often conclude that the location and growth of high-technology clusters are the result of disparate processes. Explaining their origins and growth requires highly disaggregated industry-by-industry analyses. Each cluster seems to call for a distinct explanation. Yet, our examination of the growth of high-technology activities in different regions of the Western world indicates that the processes of emergence, far from being random, exhibit clear patterns.

The Need for a Conceptual Model

The emergence of high-technology clusters is a modern version of the century-old process of economic development, described by Jane Jacobs in *The Economy of Cities* as adding new work to replace the old. In fact, high-technology clusters in the United States, Canada, and Western Europe have appeared naturally in various metropolitan areas without public strategic designs. A study of the processes by which high-technology clusters have emerged, as well as an investigation of the impact of various public policies aimed at stimulating their emergence, led us to propose a model that links several factors into dynamic processes.

Our consultation and field research in a dozen high-technology agglomerations has led us to develop an institutional approach stressing the processes accounting for new venture activities and the structural factors that support or constrain them. To understand the emergence of high-technology clusters, one has to "sin bravely" and go beyond aggregate statistical analyses. Reliance on a conceptual model that gives a coherent but experience-grounded explanation of the processes at work is necessary.

Our contention is that the emergence of a high-technology cluster in a region is heavily influenced by institutional conditions such as the diversity of the industrial base, and the availability of venture capital, and strong local leadership. In other words, the emergence of new technical activities is influenced, to a great extent, by prior conditions and processes in the region. Self-sustaining high-technology clusters result from a gradual build-up and grafting of locally initiated activities and firms. Later the processes of growth may ossify.

Our model (see figure 3–1) describes the process by which a cluster of high-technology firms emerges in the industrial base of a region. At the core of the model are "agglomeration effects" that stimulate the entrepreneurial process of starting and expanding high-technology firms. The agglomeration effects are of three types: incubation, sponsorship, and role modeling. External conditions, which will enhance or hinder them, are affected by the infrastructure: R&D, venture capital, and social support.

The supply of entrepreneurs is not an entirely independent phenomenon imputable to varying cultural norms. On the contrary, our experience indicates that entrepreneurship is widely distributed and is triggered by the proper institutional, stimulative, or permissive conditions. In some areas, this entrepreneurship is expressed in low-technology manufacturing or service industries because of the particular prevailing conditions. By contrast, the supply of technical entrepreneurship is heavily dependent on supporting processes and the institutional infrastructure.

Entrepreneurial Ventures and the Growth of High-Technology Clusters

Growth rests on entrepreneurial initiatives. Economic development is the result of the continuous, persistent grafting of new economic activities. Some of these additions, such as new shopping centers, are conventional responses to growing demand. The entrepreneur in low-technology or service industries supplies a well-known offering to match increasing demand. Other "grafts" are more innovative. The nurturing of innovative acts based upon new products or services is at the core of the economic growth process. Growth based on high technology hinges on the exploitation of market opportunities opened up by advances and diffusion of technical knowledge.

The process of economic growth stems from two "modes": the creation of new ventures and the expansion of existing firms. We will refer to the creation of new firms as the entrepreneurial mode and the initiation of new

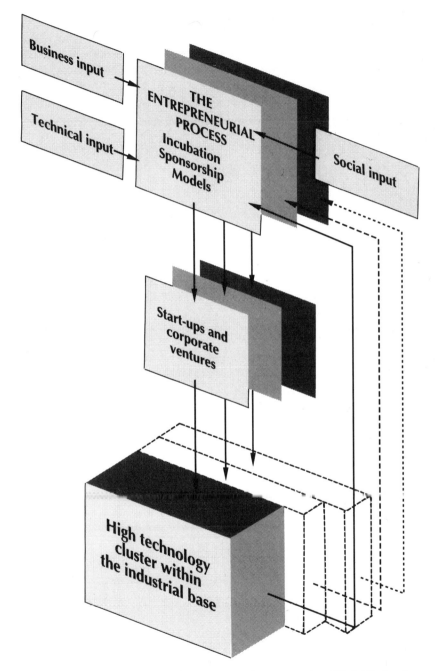

Figure 3–1. The Structure and Processes of an Emerging High-Technology Cluster

ventures by existing enterprises as the corporate mode. Entrepreneurs, who launch businesses, whether by forming independent start-ups or as internal corporate ventures, see a window of opportunity for technology-based products and services. Launching the venture is perceived as feasible because access to technical, financial, and personnel resources is possible, and because the social milieu in which entrepreneurs operate is supportive.

Joseph Schumpeter is the economist whose name is often associated with entrepreneurship. Schumpeter saw in the entrepreneurial process the main causal factor in economic growth. Schumpeter also concluded that large firms with a degree of economic power, rather than individual entrepreneurs, were to become the major source of innovation. The loss to society from weakened competition, he felt, would be compensated for by the greater gains derived from the ability of large firms to manage innovation.

Whether the major sources of innovation and new jobs are technical ventures by established corporations or small firms is an unsettled debate. Recently, numerous researchers have reemphasized the role played by entrepreneurs and small firms. We have a particular view on this subject based on the examination of technical and industrial dynamics. We believe that the issue has to be tackled on a sector basis. In some sectors, large firms are prime creators of new jobs and are innovators. In other sectors, small entrepreneurial firms are at the vanguard. In a dynamic economy, the mix of sectors is such that overall small firms create more jobs than large firms. Yet, it must be stressed that aggregate reality masks significant sectorial differences. In industries such as integrated circuits, chemicals, and mainframe computers, large firms are innovative and create jobs. In other industries, such as biomedical products or advanced manufacturing technologies, a reverse relation is observed. In many industries, entry through the creation of new firms is common. In other industries, only large firms can survive, even at the early stages of development of the technical sector.

The Entrepreneurial Mode: Start-Ups and Spin-Offs

Although many large established organizations remain innovative and change their product offerings to meet shifting demand, the record in terms of new business formation in the high-technology field seems largely to be in favor of the entrepreneurial pattern. The creation of new firms by entrepreneurs who find niches, imitate successful strategies, and undertake technical ventures to supply large firms is the major factor in the development of high-technology industries.

Contrary to what is often believed, new high-technology start-ups are quite resilient: most survive. However, only a few high-technology start-ups become high-performance firms, as measured by sales growth, profitability, and return on capital. Most high-technology firms remain small, not only because of their founders' preferences, but due to competitive and technical conditions. Economies of scale do not arise in every sector. The high survival rate of technology-based companies is most probably attributable to their flexibility and to the existence of market niches based on technical expertise.

Start-ups are usually associated with younger industries in their innovation and growth phases. These emerging industries are challenged by growing demand, discontinuous technical changes, and low levels of capital investments. This set of conditions creates low entry barriers and leads to high rates of business formation. This technical and market "effervescence" opens up multiple-specialty markets. Knowledge of these markets depends on intimate experience with firms participating in the industry. The evolution of markets creates opportunities for entrepreneur-led small firms.

Start-ups have been extremely important to the development of the minicomputer and the supercomputer industry. The first minicomputers were developed at universities such as MIT, Harvard and Pennsylvania, largely under government scientific or defense contracts. Mainframe computer manufacturers and other firms had access to the results of these research efforts. All results were public information. The founders of Digital Equipment were involved in similar contract research work. They carefully examined the TX-O computer developed at MIT on an Airforce research project and then developed the PDP, a successful mini-computer, similar to the TX-O.

Not all start-ups are pioneers and early entrants in emerging industries. Indeed, most high-technology start-ups are followers and imitators in manufacturing and service industries where barriers to entry are low. New entrants often develop market segments with intellectual and informational capital obtained from established firms. New entrants help develop overall markets by focusing on multiple segments that eventually lead to the formation of large markets.

The Corporate Mode: Venturing by Established Firms

The success of Silicon Valley and Route 128 highlights the importance of entrepreneurial start-ups as the critical mode for developing a high-technology cluster. However, effervescence in a region is also stimulated by the willingness of established business leaders to experiment with internal ventures and alliances with small firms. This corporate mode involves not only promoting internal entrepreneurship for new ventures but also engaging in strategic linkages with small firms to acquire the needed technology.

Innovative technology-based firms must modify their corporate strategies to remain entrepreneurial. Indeed, the promotion of internal entrepreneurship has become a research and action topic of great interest. Many technology-based firms have a reputation for encouraging entrepreneurship and introducing innovations. Making an established firm "entrepreneurial" has become a theme of research that overshadows the emphasis on rational corporate planning.

In spite of the difficulties of internal ventures, many technology-based firms remain the source of product innovations when their technical bases remain fecund but market structures are characterized by barriers to entry in R&D, capital, or distribution. The success record of large firms with venturing activities is mixed. Indeed the successes depend heavily on unsolicited internal proposals. But in some sectors, where few small scale entrants can make their way because of the conditions of entry, the field is open for corporate entrepreneurship.

When industries are characterized by barriers to entry and economies of scale in research, production, or distribution, established firms have a distinct information and resource advantage over small firms. For instance, the mainframe, the supercomputer, or the pharmaceutical industries, though still effervescent from a technological point of view, have remained the domain of large firms.

Many established firms have learned to intertwine technology considerations into corporate strategy. Technology strategy, which is mainly concerned with the development and acquisition of technologies to service market opportunities, used to be concerned mainly with internal R&D management or product development. However, large firms have developed relationships with entrepreneurial firms possessing specific technological skills. Research grants, contract research, collaboration agreements, equity participation, and joint ventures have been used as defensive, or pro-active, means to develop targeted technologies. As a consequence, new trends in the strategic management of technology stress diversity, venturing, and international outlook. Large firms learn to go beyond a regional outlook and develop multiple windows on technology.

The field of biotechnology has been the scene of numerous alliances between large and small firms. Developed in universities over the last forty years by extensive basic and applied research funded by the National Institute of Health, the biological sciences have experienced a radical transformation. New technologies, like genetic engineering and cell fusion, have opened up technical opportunities. Scientific entrepreneurs have launched hundreds of firms in the hope of developing pharmaceutical or agricultural products.

Many pharmaceutical, petrochemical, agri-business, and engineering firms were caught off guard. Plans for building up new internal R&D capabilities were preceded by the multiplication of alliances with universities and small firms selling research expertise. Alliances between large pharmaceutical, chemical, or agri-business firms and small entrepreneurial firms are common in the field of biotechnology. Such alliances arise because of the newness and the dynamism of biotechnologies: small entrepreneurial firms sell research services and knowledge, while large firms establish a defensive position to protect their markets or exploit new market opportunities.

These alliances are often international. Examples of agreements between firms include Zilog–NEC, Philipps–Siemens, and NEC–Tektronics. The agreements reflect a blending of technical expertise and technology-development cooperation.

In the field of electronic instruments, Analog Devices has made the funding of internal or external entrepreneurial teams and alliances with small firms key strategic means for growth. In an industry where product life cycles can be short, Analog Devices has relied not only on internal product line extensions through R&D but on internal ventures, external venture companies financed by Analog Devices, and acquisitions and investing in existing entrepreneurial firms.

Avenues of Growth of High-Technology Clusters

A typical metropolitan high-technology cluster is composed of many types of establishments. Two distinct types of strategic orientations are intermingled in a high-technology cluster. Some firms are "basic" in their market orientations, others are local. The basic group is composed of technologically-based firms that view themselves as participants in national, and even worldwide, industries: these firms are oriented toward sales outside the region. Large and small firms that form this group represent close to fifty percent of the high-technology firms in a cluster. The local group is composed of locally oriented firms. The majority of small, high-technology firms in a cluster are oriented toward the local market, where they supply other high-technology firms or offer services to established industrial or commercial firms.

Figure 3–2 describes the various avenues in the development of a high-technology cluster by externally and locally oriented firms. Externally oriented high-technology firms are based on emerging technical fields. Their growth patterns are heavily dependent on the evolution of national or international demand. Examples of such industries are pharmaceuticals, electronics, computers, semiconductors, aerospace, telecommunications, advanced manufacturing techniques, and specialized chemicals. Externally oriented firms will be large or small, depending on the particular dynamics of the high-technology sector in which they operate. The greater the diversity of high-technology industries in which firms are active, the more likely the cluster will withstand the ups and downs of market demands. Three broad avenues for the development of new activities in this part of the high-technology clusters are: the creation of new firms, the expansion of existing firms, and the establishment of branch plants.

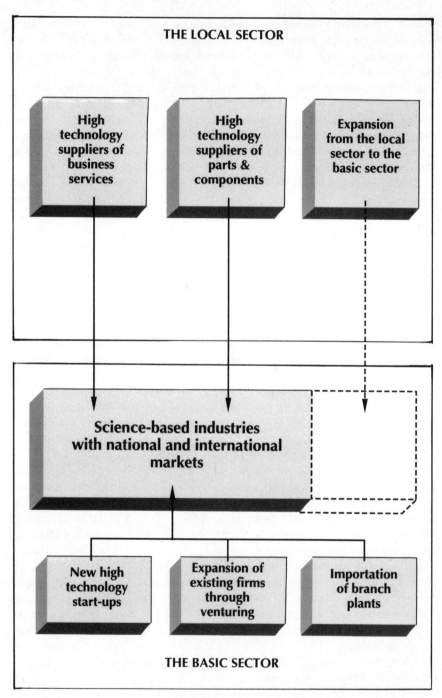

Figure 3–2. Avenues of Growth in a High-Technology Cluster

The majority of firms in a high-technology cluster are oriented toward the local market. These small firms are suppliers of parts, components, and services and depend on the economic health of the externally oriented sectors and the growth of industrial and commercial activities in the region. The demand for high-technology products and services in this local sector originates from two broad categories of firms: local capital-intensive manufacturing corporations that need to adopt new manufacturing techniques to remain competitive, and local commercial financial and service businesses that need to adapt to opportunities in using telecommunication, information, and computer technologies. New high-technology activities in the local sector will arise from the establishment of local suppliers of parts and components and the creation of service-oriented firms. A fraction of locally oriented high-technology firms will eventually transform themselves into externally oriented producers.

Let us examine the four avenues of growth of high-technology activities that will be established in response to market opportunities in the local service or manufacturing sectors and in industries for which markets are national or international in scope.

Creating New Ventures in Emerging Science-Based Sectors

The creation of new ventures in an emerging field of science is usually what gives a cluster a reputation for high-technology effervescence. The presence of incubating organizations from which spin-offs emerge within a particular region can be the result of chance or design; for instance, Shockley Laboratories in Palo Alto, Lincoln Laboratories in Cambridge, ERA in the Twin Cities, and Bell Northern Research in Ottawa located where they did as much because of random events as because of previous public and private investments in the regional technical infrastructure.

A region may house a few technology-based organizations at a time when international and national demands for these products begin to grow. For example, the growth of firms in the fields of supercomputers in Minneapolis, integrated circuits in Palo Alto, and advanced manufacturing in Torino is highly dependent on increasing demand in these particular industries. In the first few years of the emergence of a new industry, a few independent organizations are created either as spin-offs or as creative imitations. The products of these firms are not sold locally but mostly to manufacturing or service firms located in other industrial or high-technology agglomerations.

As demand firms up for a particular type of product in an emerging field, a few initial start-ups are established. A period of gestation and learning follows during which the rate of business creation is still low. If, however, the sectors in which the firms operate experience sustained demand as a result of a variety of opportunities in niches, a period of acceleration growth follows in which the rate of business creation increases. Eventually as opportunities diminish the barriers to entry rise, the rate of business formation dwindles.

The events that trigger the launching of businesses may be viewed in a positive fashion as the "pull of opportunities." Entrepreneurs identify market niches for which they possess the required technical resources. Such opportunities may have been rejected by the former corporations in which entrepreneurs worked. Furthermore, barriers to entry into the industry may be low. As an indication of the pull of opportunities, SRI International (formerly the Stanford Research Institute) has never been able to organize a coherent and forceful program in biotechnology because key staff members leave to pursue opportunities identified in the course of contract research activities.

Negative focus also lead to new business creations. The high probability of contract termination for engineers and scientists working in applied research institutions is a common problem for defense and aerospace suppliers or university-related contract research organizations. As a consequence, scientists and engineers are constantly on the look-out for opportunities. The frustrations experienced by many would-be entrepreneurs in large corporations in which strategic requirements and bureaucratic modes of operations are seen as constraining, may also push for independent breakaways.

A number of small high-technology clusters have emerged in England around large technology-based firms such as Ferranti, Plessy, Vickers, and Rolls-Royce. These firms were rich in technology but highly focused on existing product lines. In difficult times, many engineers, scientists, and marketing executives were fired. These persons dropped into the local fabric and used the existing local infrastructure to start up companies using the leading technologies they had worked on. Former employers were sometimes hostile, but many eventually asked these newly created firms to become suppliers.

Genealogical links are sometimes quite visible when the emerging technical sector is experiencing high market demand and low barriers to entry. For instance, many generations of firms have been spawned by Engineering Research Associates, which was set up in 1946 in St. Paul to undertake contract work on computing machines. As the computer industry gained credibility and as demand increased, the flow of start-ups linked to ERA grew. ERA was purchased in 1952 by Remington Rand, which merged with Sperry Corporation in 1955. The Sperry-Univac division was established to manufacture computers and peripheral equipment. Several spin-offs from this division occurred in the late 1950s and early 1960s. Figure 3–3 shows the major entities derived from ERA up to 1983.

Expanding Existing Technologically Based Firms

Corporate ventures and expansion projects also contribute to the birth of new high-technology activities. The growth potential of established firms depends upon a wide variety of factors: their products, their markets, and their management.

As a general rule, the potential for growth varies inversely with the age of firms. The potential for growth is higher for a young enterprise than for an older one. Studies by David Birch confirm that an overwhelming majority of new jobs are created by establishments that are four years old or younger, because the pressure for growth tends to diminish as professional managers settle in.

The growth potential of a firm is also linked to its innovativeness. A company that is thirty-years-old with a work force that has expanded little, or not at all, generally offers a poor potential for growth. In fact, it is unlikely that a firm in a state of relative stagnation would suddenly rediscover the elements necessary for a resumption of growth. A stagnant company becomes out-of-date with regard to its products, image, technology, equipment, and competence of its personnel. Stable firms are among the least likely to expand and the most likely to fail.

The management team also makes a real difference. A firm that displays sustained growth is often managed by a team that has both the willingness and the capacity to develop the firm. This willingness and capacity vary considerably from one firm to the other, and even with time within the firm. The swiftness with which management includes technology in corporate strategy or promotes internal ventures determines whether established firms will play a role in regional high-technology development.

The major means by which established corporations contribute to the growth of a high-technology cluster include the following.

Research and Development. Firms with a fruitful technical base can invest a substantial proportion of their revenues to generate a stream of technical and market ideas. Shifts to new technical bases through extensive R&D efforts allow firms to face technical and market discontinuities.

Market research techniques and deliberate approaches to opportunity identification, product design, testing, and product introduction have significantly reduced new product failures. Market information is extremely valuable for reducing probabilities of failure at the different stages of product development. Success is usually associated with superior products, well-targeted market studies, and proficiency in product design, development, and launching.

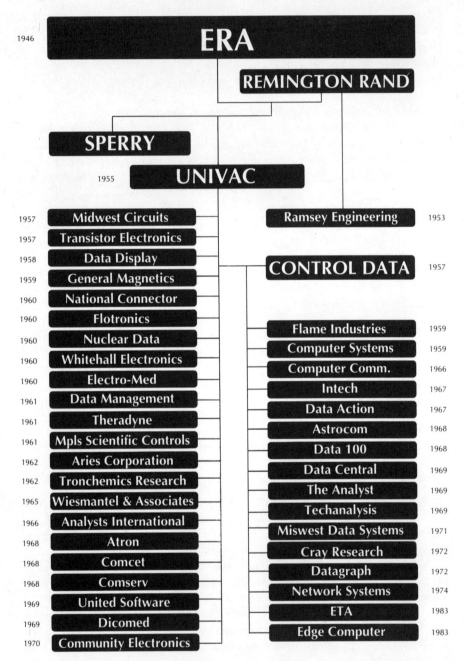

Figure 3–3. ERA and Its Spin-offs

Internal Ventures and Voluntary Spin-Offs. Internal ventures refer to the establishment of distinct entities for the purpose of entering new markets or developing new products. Internal venturing is based as often on strategic choices as on unsolicited initiatives from subordinates. Internal venturing often requires a culture and an organization design that stimulate and reward entrepreneurial behavior.

Voluntary spin-offs of existing firms refer to the internal development of venture projects and their eventual incorporation as independent firms. Technology transfer and ownership arrangements are established prior to the sale of equity to former employees or business partners.

Joint Ventures and Alliances. Joint ventures and alliances with small firms for the development of new technical capabilities and for entry into new industries are also used by large firms. Small partners with experience in emerging technical fields are sought. For instance, many large firms have reacted with defensive ventures and alliances to emerging technologies by keeping abreast of new firms and their technologies. Some firms have learned to combine internal product development with alliances with small technology-based firms.

Acquisitions. The basis of this strategy is the acquisition of successful high-technology firms by mature corporations wishing to enter new technical sectors. A substantial proportion of new start-ups are acquired by established firms. An appropriate diversification strategy will focus on technologies or families of technologies that are in the growth phase of development.

Strategic reorientations of firms into emerging industries are difficult to achieve. Mature firms can be very effective in launching improved products and innovative processes based on known technologies. In certain fields, large firms can successfully invade industries where barriers to entry exclude small entrants. However, being successful at venturing into new fields where small firms can operate is another matter.

Importing Branch Plants and Regional Offices

High-technology firms are quite often composed of multiple establishments. Research activities are usually located near headquarters, while production activities are spread out from the original core into low-cost areas. As a rule, branch plants are not the basis upon which the development of a self-sustaining high-technology cluster is articulated. Branch plants are not likely to lead to technologically based spin-offs because their managers are seldom exposed to the market place and to the difficulties of product design. Moreover, the production-oriented work environment is not conducive to entrepreneurial initiatives by employees.

However, there have been exceptional cases where an agglomeration of branch plants has established the conditions for the emergence of a self-sustaining cluster. Central Scotland, the Research Triangle Park, and West London are examples of growing clusters where established firms have set-up autonomous divisions, regional headquarters, and world-mandate manufacturing plants.

Consider the case of West London. This high-technology agglomeration along the M3-M4 motorways owes its origins to the warehouses and European-headquarters offices of U.S. computer manufacturers built around Heathrow Airport during the 1950s and early 1960s. These unplanned events laid the foundation for a spontaneous and unexpected growth process. Firms moved to the area because of its convenient access to suppliers, the airport, and customers. In fact, firms refused incentives to locate elsewhere. The area expanded and still does at the rate of half a mile per year. The road and infrastructure were present. A highly qualified staff was also available due to the presence of training and manufacturing facilities established during World War II.

Meeting Local Demand for Products and Services

After a sufficient number of establishments have been set up as start-ups, corporate new ventures or branch plants, local subcontracting, and complementary markets begin to appear. High-technology goods or services are produced locally when local demand ensures the minimum level of operation to allow competitive efficiency. As a region's economy grows, there are always new economic activities that pass the threshold level of profitability for local production. Entrepreneurs are continuously on the watch for these opportunities and will test the market place. Start-ups oriented toward the local market are launched as opportunities unfold. Relying on local start-ups for specialized sourcing is risky, but proximity makes close monitoring of suppliers possible and compensates for the risks of experimentation. Similarly, an agglomeration of growing high-technology firms can provide the specialized, but thin, markets for the technical entrepreneurs who start locally oriented firms. Our studies indicate that more than half of the high-technology firms in any particular cluster are oriented toward the local market. A few of these firms will eventually outgrow their regional orientation to become exporters.

The growth of local or "metropolitan" activities in manufacturing or financial services also leads to a demand for high-technology services. Companies will be created to offer services in data processing, information systems, advanced manufacturing, and computer aided design. The business of these service-oriented companies is the diffusion of existing early stage technologies. For instance, the diffusion of advanced manufacturing techniques or office automation processes will open up opportunities for specialized firms. Every metropolitan and regional agglomeration has a large number of computer consultants, software services, and specialized laboratories that service mostly the local market.

A Typology of High-Technology Clusters

Figure 3–4 shows a typology that was developed to account for the variety of technology clusters. Four basic types of clusters have been identified by using a combination of two fundamental characteristics: the diversity of the industrial structure and the entrepreneurial character of the cluster. The first axis indicates the diversity of high-technology activities in the infrastructure. One pole is oriented toward diversity in the infrastructure and the other toward a narrow or focused high-technology infrastructure. The second axis describes the forces by which the cluster grows. The first pole is mainly through home-grown entrepreneurial start-ups and spin-offs while the other is through the establishment of plants by large corporations or government research institutions.

Four types of high-technology clusters can thus be identified: self-sustaining, dependent research, technology fabrication, and focused.

Self-sustaining clusters have both a diversified high-technology infrastructure and the agglomeration economies that lead to a high rate of local business formation. Examples are Route 128, Silicon Valley, Minneapolis, Los Angeles, and West London.

Dependent research clusters are rich, diverse, but stagnant technical agglomerations that depend on continued government or corporate sponsored research activities. A few high-technology firms may emerge but a self-sustaining process is never triggered. Examples are West Berkshire in England, Washington, D.C., and Sheridan Park in Toronto. Many dependent research clusters were born as planned technology parks.

Fabrication-oriented clusters are on the low end of high technology. Many branch plants are established due to the availability of staff and public incentives. Such clusters may open opportunities for new businesses by focusing mostly on local supply. Examples are found in Central Scotland, New Hampshire, and the Bromont area southeast of Montreal. Fabrication-oriented clusters rarely become effectively self-sustaining as the experience of the Research Triangle Park shows.

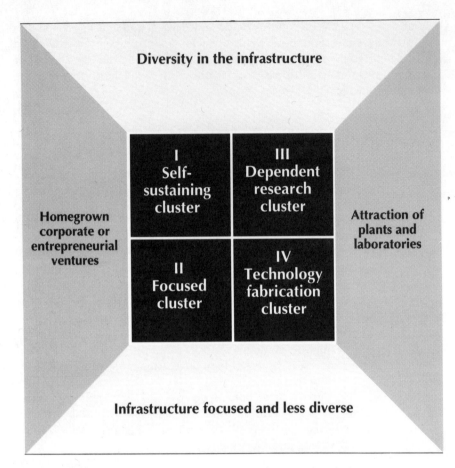

Figure 3–4. A Typology of High-Technology Clusters

Focused clusters derive from a few high-technology sectors serving mostly large local industrial needs. The high-technology base is diluted in a mature industrial agglomeration. Examples of such clusters are found in Detroit, Torino, and Pittsburgh.

Our main interest is in the self-sustaining clusters and the means by which an emerging cluster becomes self-sustaining. Thus, the conceptual framework discussed in the next chapter will focus on self-sustaining clusters.

4
The Entrepreneurial Process in Self-Sustaining Clusters

To the casual observer, technical entrepreneurs are risk takers, even gamblers, who stake their future on dreams. But in their opinion, entrepreneurs do not take major risks. They know (and strongly believe) that they possess unique competitive and information advantages. Furthermore, the determination to leverage these advantages into ventures is expected to be amply rewarded.

Traditional conceptions of entrepreneurs emphasize risk taking and individual action. Contacts with technical entrepreneurs rapidly reveal that they are not risk takers but determined individuals with high needs for achievement who rely on the resources that the environment provides. Most entrepreneurs are motivated by the desire to prove that they are capable of getting results and by the need to be recognized by peers. Some have lofty ideals such as applying the talents they have received to serve the common good. However, research on the sociopsychological characteristics of entrepreneurs has not been very successful in identifying universal traits, styles, or personality characteristics associated with entrepreneurship. Entrepreneurship, it seems, is highly contingent upon the social and economic context.

Our argument is that technical entrepreneurship flourishes in regions where the decision to launch a technology-based company is perceived as a low risk by the entrepreneurs. Such a context arises because highly valuable and risk-reducing information is available to technical entrepreneurs. In deciding to profit from these opportunities, technical entrepreneurs know they operate with privileged information and a headstart.

Risk reducing and obtaining valuable information result from three major processes in the region: the incubation experience leading to the discovery of opportunities; the stimulation of a rich commercial environment, providing business contacts and resources; and the entrepreneurial and management guidance offered by models.

Technical entrepreneurs identify market opportunities and notice ways of exploiting them in the course of their early work experience in incubator organizations. However, identifying highly valuable opportunities is not enough. Resources and information are needed to make the venture feasible. Strategies to get the required resources and build the organization to pursue desirable opportunities depend on the perceived feasibility of this entrepreneurial act. Role models offered by successful entrepreneurs provide information on ways and means to launch a start-up and manage a growing firm. Finally, the successful launching of a business will depend on the resources that are made available to entrepreneurs in the form of business contracts and financing.

The creation and clustering of high-technology firms are supported by these enabling processes. In this chapter, we will review the incubation process, the importance of sponsorship, the influence of successful role models, and the agglomeration effects.

The Incubation Process

Incubators are organizations which are closely associated with the origin and the early growth of start-ups. They provide would-be entrepreneurs with jobs before they launch their own business. While working in incubating milieus, entrepreneurs have access to highly valuable information about market and technical opportunities that is available at low or no cost. Moreover, job tenure allows would-be entrepreneurs to establish their reputation vis-á-vis potential partners, clients, suppliers, distributors, and venture capitalists.

Exposure to best-practice technology also makes it possible for entrepreneurs to uncover business opportunities based on novel applications. Intimate knowledge of markets gives entrepreneurs the chance to make the contacts that are vital for identifying niches and opportunities. This in-depth understanding of the marketplace is essential for new product success. Access to this information is most likely to be available to somebody working in a corporation already active in a high-technology sector. Unambiguous feedback in the form of changes in market shares or ambiguous feedback in the form of hints and clues from product difficulties, competitors' activities, or basic research direct would-be entrepreneurs' attention and creative abilities toward better product alternatives and business opportunities.

The histories of successful entrepreneurs show that nearly all technical entrepreneurs had a number of years of scientific research or engineering experience before formulating their venture concepts. During their participation in product innovations or internal ventures, engineers and scientists encounter and solve development problems that lead to market opportunities. Sometimes these opportunities are left unexploited by incubator organizations.

Some types of firms and industries tend to be more effective than others in breeding new ventures or independent firms. Within industries, firms also vary in their ability to spawn new start-ups. Four types of effective incubators may be distinguished.

Rapidly Growing High-Technology Firms

High-technology firms perturbed by rapid growth are the most effective incubators both in terms of quality and quantity. Growing high-technology organizations operate at the frontiers of knowledge and are active in the early phases of their industry. Rapid shifts in the market acceptance of competing designs require planning for new products and thus expose key personnel to competing concepts and technologies. The selection of designs often leads to frustrations, disagreements, and departures. Moreover, the high-technology firms often develop entrepreneurial cultures characterized by decentralized decision-making, creative management, and strong entrepreneurial characters.

Incubators of technical entrepreneurs often tend to be small but growing companies. Indeed, the most effective incubators are usually growing high-technology firms perturbed by the flu, pains, and decisions of rapid growth. Rapid shifts in the market acceptance of competing designs require planning for new products and thus expose key personnel to competing concepts and technologies.

A few years of work experience in such incubating firms open avenues to potential entrepreneurs. Some incubators will prevent entrepreneurs from launching their own business: many incubators simply lose high-potential employees. Bell Northern Research has been a prime incubator for high-technology entrepreneurs in the Ottawa and Montreal area. Over 100 start-ups, such as Mitel or Orchatech, were launched by technical entrepreneurs trained and even supported by Bell Northern Research.

Mature Firms Undergoing Change

Mature technology-based firms form the second most important type of incubators. These firms are not based on emerging technologies. However, they need to constantly adopt best-practice methods to stay competitive. Mature technology-based firms deal with horizontal state-of-the-art technologies to improve the competitiveness of their operations. Would-be entrepreneurs are initiated to technologies that are in the early stages of diffusion. Drug companies, airplane makers, and office equipment manufacturers are often involved in state-of-the-art telecommunications, computer-aided design/computer-aided manufacturing (CAD/CAM), microelectronics, and fermentation technologies. A substantial fraction of start-ups can be traced to such technology-based but mature firms.

Many mature technology-based companies are investing heavily in new or embryonic technical fields to solve technological bottlenecks affecting current production systems or as defensive moves against technological threats. For instance, Bell Laboratories saw in solid-state physics the possibility of developing a superior alternative to the troublesome vacuum-tube amplifier. Major breakthroughs occur at their R&D labs, but these firms are often unable to move rapidly into markets. Soon scientists and engineers leave these firms in frustration to join other faster-moving concerns or to start their own.

Xerox's attempt to diversify from its copier line to the "electronic office of the future" is an example of the difficulties that technology-based firms face. In order to achieve this diversification effort, Xerox set up, in 1970, its Palo Alto Research Center (PARC), and assigned it the goal of generating the technology of the electronic office. Years later, PARC has become a mecca for talented researchers, and an embarrassment. For the hundred of millions spent, Xerox has reaped far less than it expected. Yet technical entrepreneurs have turned the ideas born there into start-up companies.

Regional Headquarters

Regional headquarters that house marketing, product development, and production activities may, over the years, become incubators as they combine all the critical functions that provide potential entrepreneurs with much of the needed information to start a venture. On the other hand, most branch plants are sterile as incubators, as they do not interchange with the market place.

Contract Research Organizations

Contract research organizations and consulting firms serve as stepping stones to start-ups by employees, since employment in institutions like Draper Laboratories is often highly contingent upon projects that have a limited lifespan. As projects appear to approach completion, employees are often on the lookout for technical and market opportunities that may lead to the launching of a venture.

Some organizations are not as effective as incubators. We already mentioned manufacturing branch plants. Government research centers and universities also do not provide much exposure to market opportunities on which viable ventures can be built.

Indeed, in spite of well-known cases of professors successfully starting businesses, the facts do not substantiate the hypothesis that high-technology firms grow out of university laboratories and industry-university research centers. The majority of technical spin-offs from universities have, in fact, originated in contract research centers or applied laboratories rather than in scientific departments. Moreover, technical start-ups are associated with only a handful of institutions of learning in the United States, Canada, and Western Europe. Universities have seldom been the direct source of high-technology firms, in spite of extensive efforts in terms of research parks and programs directed to commercial product development.

For instance, Technology Square was established as an incubating organization set up by MIT with the expectation that faculty members and graduate students would establish their start-up firms needing space close to the university and its laboratories, at least during their start-up phase. To the chagrin of promoters, it was found that entrepreneurs starting businesses were mostly former employees of firms already located in the suburbs, and they also preferred to set up shop in suburban locations.

The policies and practices of effective incubator organizations socialize would-be entrepreneurs to values, aspirations, and technical skills critical for spin-offs or internal ventures. Potential entrepreneurs learn the necessary managerial skills and the dynamics of the industry through first-hand experience. In fact, the product–market strategy the technical entrepreneurs use is often learned and determined by interactions with the experts and the customers of the incubator organization.

Genealogical links are sometimes quite visible from high-profile incubators when an emerging technical sector is experiencing high demand. For instance, William Shockley, the inventor of the transistor, returned to Palo Alto, his home town, to establish Shockley Laboratories. A few years later, some employees left to found Fairchild Industries. In the 1960s, spin-offs from Fairchild lead to the birth of INTEL, National Semiconductor, and Advanced Micro Devices, which become second order spin-offs. In the same fashion, many incubator organizations account for the budding or high-technology firms in the Boston area in the 1950s. Raytheon, Sperry Rand, and General Electric were the major original incubators.

The presence of incubators attracts and locates technical would-be entrepreneurs in specific regions. Thus, incubators play a determining role in the physical location of new firms. The networks that entrepreneurs have developed are bound to the environment of their incubator. Most entrepreneurs elect to start their businesses in the area where they work and where their contacts are developed. The successful launching of new technical ventures is heavily dependent on such personal and friendly relations.

Thus, the more incubators in a region, the higher the chances of spin-offs and start-ups in the area. By contrast, a region that hosts few incubators will not generate many new firms. Incubator organizations may ossify and lose their original abilities to introduce potential entrepreneurs to opportunities. When such events occur, the region loses much of its dynamism.

Sponsorship

As the number of high-tech establishments grows and as some firms become successful, a rich and stimulating commercial environment takes shape in a region. Established firms that are dependent on state-of-the-art technologies, whether they are prime military contractors, computer manufacturers, or service companies such as stock brokers, banks, or insurance companies, act as sponsors or stimulators for the creation of new businesses.

Entrepreneurs pursue opportunities without regard to resources currently controlled by them. They are after opportunities, and these opportunities frame their needs for resources. Technical entrepreneurs seldom find that current resources of their disposal are entirely appropriate. However, they will rely on the environment in which they operate to provide them with these resources, which include capital, space, personnel, and business contracts. Finding commercial "sponsors" in the local economic fabric is critical to the success of start-ups. This section will discuss the sponsorship activities as well as network building which makes launching a business feasible. (The issues of venture capital and business advice will be discussed in the next chapter.)

Initial Contracts

A stimulating environment offers initial contracts that help entrepreneurs set up their businesses. Every entrepreneur remembers his first contract. The framed dollar bill hanging on the wall behind the cash register is more than an act of folklore: it documents a critical moment in any new corporation, its first sale, which by any standard, is not a "normal" sale. Buying from a newcomer is not the same as buying from an established corporation. This is why it is called "sponsoring." Especially in the area of high technology, being among the first purchasers from a new high-technology company requires a good amount of faith. These first buyers are often mature companies. In that role, they play a key function in either triggering new firms or preventing them. Why, or in which circumstances, will companies or governments contract with new firms?

The prevailing corporate culture often dictates that greater economies of scale can be achieved through vertical integration. Such policies work against experimentation that can support the development of new firms. However, many firms rely on specialized and low-cost suppliers. Contracting-out gives them greater mobility and access to new technologies.

A study of over 100 start-ups in the Montreal region indicates that in half of the cases, the founders could identify the awarding of an initial contract (mostly by local firms) as the critical event leading to the birth of their venture. Firms that played such a stimulating or sponsoring role were not always technology-based firms. Indeed, the majority consisted of banks, insurance companies, broadcasters, and utilities.

Many established firms routinely engage in collaborative ventures with smaller high-technology start-ups. IBM, for instance, opens up its client base to firms with specialized software. Initial markets for new technical ventures may thus be provided by mature technology-based firms. Their role as initial customers will be greater if they encourage experimentation and have positive attitudes toward new products and new processes suggested by suppliers.

Complex networks of interactions over time are involved in the emergence of an industry. As an indication of the supporting linkages between large and small firms in the development of a technical field, let us take the example of CAD/CAM technologies. In the late 1950s, innovative executives in aerospace and integrated circuits firms visualized the potential applications of computer and graphics technologies to their production processes. General Motors instigated the first industrial application of CAD with its "design augmented by computers" (DAC) program, beginning in 1959. Similar programs were developed at Lockheed and McDonnell. These pioneering firms trained software writers who were instrumental in the formation of many of the CAD start-ups in the 1960s, as well as in the development of the basic graphics software which these firms used. University-related laboratories, such as MIT, and a few firms were granted contracts to develop the techniques and train the highly skilled people needed for their applications. Spin-offs appeared in the late 1960s by entrepreneurs who had experience with users and developers of the technology. Sales in the CAD/CAM industry are now around five-billion dollars world-wide.

The presence of experienced suppliers of components, mechanical parts, and programming services, also reduces the risk for technical start-ups. Entrepreneurial firms can contract-out for suppliers and thus focus their energies on designing and building the products on which their future depends. This phenomenon of uncertainty reduction is especially evident for electronic, biomedical and instrument manufacturers who can take for granted the presence of highly qualified suppliers. In the same fashion, established firms such as aerospace or computer manufacturers can design innovative products with the certainty that highly qualified suppliers will be available.

Governments also play a key role in stimulating the growth of technology-based firms through military and space research. Studies of the impact of government support on the electronic industry has confirmed the importance of research and procurement contracts. Defense procurement and support for R&D had a major impact on the microelectronics industry, mainly through the sponsoring of new firms and ventures. R&D contracts awarded to established firms also increased the performance and reliability of products. Direct purchases, proposals, and research contracts served as a basis to assist the entry of new firms as spin-offs from established firms or university laboratories. Start-ups entered the industry at the moment of high learning and were thus able to survive and focus rapidly on industrial and consumer markets.

On a regional level, governments or companies can make a real difference. For example, Montreal is home to three of the world's ten largest engineering firms, mainly as a result of Hydro Quebec's commitment to contracting out. Having built up capacity to perform major civil engineering work locally, these firms later scouted the world for contracts. Today, these firms are diversifying into production of high-technology products linked to their expertise. Conversely, the policy at Ontario Hydro has been not to contract-out. Instead, in-house engineering capabilities were developed in the nuclear field. Today, this Ontario Hydro department does not operate at the fullest of its technical capacity, and few spin-offs occurred.

Networks

A stimulating and rich environment is also one in which networks make access to resources feasible. Once opportunities have been identified, entrepreneurs tap or develop networks to identify the resources that are necessary for start-up. Contacts are made with partners to form a sound team and with external advisors and potential buyers of the product or service. Networks of persons who are not financially linked to a new venture but offer support include business acquaintances, friends, previous employers, accountants, and government officials.

Entrepreneurs can line up in advance the external support and connections so that during start-up efforts, resources will be available. The careful selection of outsiders such as bankers, lawyers, board of directors, and informal advisors is vital to growing a successful venture. Skillful use of professional advisors can make it easier to get along with fewer full-time, paid experts. The more successful entrepreneurs have skills in using external professional resources such as consultants in developing a market niche and the specific products for their firms.

Networks of entrepreneurs are characterized by the extensiveness of ties, the paths for reaching out, and the presence of intermediaries. Successful entrepreneurs are connected to the diverse information sources that a rich and stimulating milieu provides. The speed at which contact networks are developed depends on the credibility of entrepreneurs as business persons and their skills in accessing the network of contacts. However, progress in establishing credibility is usually not made until a well thought-out business plan has been developed. Rapport is often established by stressing commonality of background (experience, schooling, training, ethnic origin, family, religion, and hobbies) and by seeking advice. The most successful entrepreneurs tend to use a broad network, which includes suppliers and potential customers.

Successful Role Models

Exposing success models to would-be entrepreneurs and to venture capitalists, buyers, and bankers helps to accelerate the rate of business creation. Success models convey highly pertinent information for strategic decision making to all parties involved in new ventures. In particular, technical entrepreneurs have before their eyes examples of opportunities, solutions to problems, and management styles that worked. Thus, models of successful start-ups provide strong stimuli to would-be entrepreneurs and act as risk reducers.

Models of successful action transmit free information about what works and what does not to those who are called upon to assist entrepreneurs in their ventures. In particular, suppliers of capital are privy to this information. Thus, a hospitable business climate for entrepreneurs can be readily established by the diffusion of success stories.

Personal contacts with successful entrepreneurs can also stimulate potential entrepreneurs who have already identified opportunities. David Offendahl, the president of ZYCAD, a Minneapolis-based manufacturer of peripherals, used to work in the technology transfer division of Control Data. His work put him in contact with entrepreneurs. He discovered that successful entrepreneurs are not extraordinary persons, but rather, determined individuals who "put on their pants just like everybody else, one leg at a time." These contacts convinced him that he had the ability to start his own venture. He proved he could by successfully launching ZYCAD.

Success models are strong stimuli for potential entrepreneurs in incubator firms. These successes suggest that partners can be found, that capital can be raised, and that "now" is perhaps the time to "do it." Information that some market opportunities did not materialize is practical "market research." In fact, the diffusion of unsuccessful models also teaches the dos and the don'ts of starting-up a new company. Finally, by making successful entrepreneurs into local heroes, models shape the values of the business and technical communities.

Success models stress the importance of team building in the start-up process. The creation of a start-up is seldom an individual enterprise. It is a joint network building achievement that centers on the inception, diffusion, and adoption of a set of ideas among a group of partners and supporters who become sufficiently committed to those ideas to transform them into an enterprise.

Models also reduce the perceived risk levels of start-up operations. Pertinent information and credibility of certain sectors for strategic decision-making is thus conveyed to the relevant players other than entrepreneurs: venture capitalists, suppliers, customers, and buyers. The progressive impact of success models proceeds through direct accounts by the media of successful attempts and informally through exchanges between entrepreneurs, venture capitalists, and bankers. Reducing uncertainty by conveying hard information on what is feasible, how it is done, and what is needed greatly facilitates the start-up process.

Agglomeration Effects

The process of incubation, sponsorship, and role models provide appropriate information and strategic guidance to potential entrepreneurs. As the number of incubators, venturesome buyers, and success models increase, agglomeration effects appear. The processes of agglomeration feed upon themselves. Thus the more incubators, the richer the environment. And the greater the number of role models, the higher the rate of high-technology business formation. By contrast, regions with few incubators, role models, or industrial sponsors will have a low rate of high-technology business formation.

Let us summarize the nature of these agglomeration effects.

Technical entrepreneurs can develop opportunities because they appropriate to themselves market and technical information that they gather in the course of their employment in incubator organizations.

A region known for the excellence of its universities and the dynamism of its high-technology firms will attract highly qualified staff that becomes available to growing firms. Firms do not have to invest as much in training but they profit from prior investment of individuals and by former employers.

The clustering of suppliers of parts, components, and services in a high technology will reduce the cost of starting and managing a new venture. Technical entrepreneurs will find readily available materials and skills that they otherwise would have to finance. This availability increases their flexibility to adapt to changing market needs.

The presence of numerous high-technology suppliers in in an area reduces the cost of subcontracting, accessing to highly specialized unbundled products, and forming strategic alliances. In other words, established firms can develop strategies of de-integration that rely on market relationships and low transaction costs.

Complementary and thin specialized markets will develop as a high-technology sector grows in a region. For instance, opportunities in visual identification, software products, or specialized industrial applications appear as a result of the growth of supercomputers in the Minneapolis/St. Paul region.

The greater the resources available in a region, the more entrepreneurs will be able to pursue opportunities while relying on external rather than owned resources. Entrepreneurs will be able to structure deals with buyers, venture capitalists, and suppliers that maximize flexibility and reduce risks.

A rich milieu will develop formal as well as informal networks through which information on entrepreneurs, technologies and business opportunities will flow easily. As information on the ways and means of high-technology start-up is diffused to venture capitalists, industrial buyers, the financial community, and business executives, the psychological cost of doing transactions is reduced.

Success models, including failures, are influencing the attitudes of persons who can help reduce the difficulties of starting or managing a high-technology start-up.

These agglomeration effects influence the location of new high-technology activities. Newly created firms tend to be located close to the entrepreneurs' homes. Normally, entrepreneurs will locate their firms in the area where they have developed contacts with future customers, venture capitalists, and suppliers. Only rarely do founders or entrepreneurs move to a new area, where they are not known, when establishing their ventures. (Indeed, just the need to preserve his borrowing capabilities, by keeping his present house and maintaining his present network of referrals, is usually sufficient to "freeze" an entrepreneur at his home base when he is launching his venture.)

Within a region, entrepreneurs will show preferences. They tend to pick speculative buildings located in suburban parks. Such suburban locations offer them reasonable cost space (downtown locations are expensive) while, at the same time, providing strong visual identity to their emerging firms. Proximity to a university is not usually a critical factor for start-ups. Contrary to common wisdom, founders do not necessarily look for cheap space, unless extensive assembly manufacturing is undertaken. Knowledge-based and image conscious firms will prefer competitively priced space that provides a strong visual identity. The real estate industry response has been to develop "office-showroom" buildings in suburban parks to meet this demand.

Fast-growing firms will locate in areas that not only promote visual identity and flexibility to expand, but are easily accessible to employees and have room for expansion. As a consequence, fast-growing firms will again prefer suburban locations where traffic is light and where ample space is available for expansion and parking. In the early stages, a firm will share a building with other tenants. Eventually, fast-growing firms move away from multitenant buildings into stand-alone properties designed to their own specifications.

The decision to locate a branch plant is based on different criteria. Having access to skilled personnel and being "where the action is" are important decision criteria, especially for the fast-growing firm that is building its first major branch plant. Economic considerations play a larger role where firms build numerous branch plants according to blue-print technologies. The location of branch plants of a corporation in the process of expansion is influenced by factors such as traveling proximity, availability of low-cost labor, and access to freeways.

Decisions to locate a research laboratory in a specific area are often affected by "political" factors. This is usually the case of government-funded laboratories. Corporations are also sometimes subjected to political pressure while locating their laboratories. The preference of a chief executive officer is to locate corporate laboratories near critical operations of the corporation, to ensure better internal communications. There is also a clear tendency for research centers of firms in the same industry to cluster in the same region. Thus, pharmaceutical laboratories are found in Philadelphia, defense and aerospace around Los Angeles, and so forth.

Conclusion

The three processes of incubation, sponsorship, and appearance of success models are enriched and spurred by agglomeration effects. High-value information is available at a low cost when a region hosts a number of leading-edge firms and when the high-technology community is rich in interactions. Despite the progress of telecommunication and data processing technologies, there is little doubt that agglomeration effects in a metropolitan region still play a large role in the emergence of high-technology clusters.

5

The Infrastructure to Support the Entrepreneurial Process

The infrastructure of a region influences the processes of incubation, sponsorship, and success models that give rise to agglomeration effects. The infrastructure constitutes the stock of institutions and resources that a region has at its disposal to develop high-technology activities. The infrastructure may be thin, as in regions that only recently saw high-technology as a mode of growth, or it may be rich, as in the case of regions where the leadership of past generations has built research oriented universities, an industrial base, and venturesome financial institutions.

A recent report by the Office of Technology Assessment indicates that regions without the adequate infrastructure cannot hope to develop high-technology activities easily. For instance, a region with a growing number of firms at the leading edge of technology and a thriving metropolitan sector will offer many initial markets. By contrast, a region with a dominance of mature firms and branch plants in diversified industrial sectors may be high in economic efficiency but low in technical venture potential.

We have identified three major groups of elements that form the infrastructure supporting the development of high-technology activities: business, technical, and social inputs. Together, they constitute the milieu in which high technology will develop. Some milieus will be richer than others, and high technology will flourish as the agglomeration effects feed on the appropriate inputs. In other milieus, a major deficiency in the infrastructure will hinder the agglomeration effects and prevent the entrepreneurial process from taking hold. Let us look at these elements.

Business Inputs

A first set of structural conditions that can accelerate the development of a high-technology cluster is the availability of business input, namely managerial advice and venture capital. These are provided to entrepreneurs through informal or formal channels, usually on the basis of a financial participation in the new ventures by outsiders. The sources of initial financing for high technology start-ups are varied. However, the critical role that informal and formal venture capital play is worth stressing.

The presence of institutionalized venture capital in a region is not essential to technological entrepreneurship. Yet, given the presence of technical entrepreneurs, nothing affects the local development of high-technology activities more than the effective availability of managerial advice and capital from investors, who validate ideas through a business plan, offer initial financing, and provide on-going support for young and growing firms. In the absence of formal, institutionalized venture capital, the availability to entrepreneurs of a network of informal investors and advisors who will examine proposals and refer them to the appropriate initial financing sources is critical for the start-up process. (In particular, valid opportunities can be channeled to investors through referrals by lawyers, accountants, bankers, and acquaintances.)

It would be a mistake to think that venture capitalists are associated with the formation of most high-technology start-ups. In fact, most start-ups develop without any input by established venture capitalists. Only 10 to 15 percent, at the most, of new businesses in high technology are financed by the formal venture capital industry. In reality, "informal" venture capitalists play an equally important role in new high-technology ventures. According to Albert Shapero, these are the sources of initial financial support for high-technology start-ups: personal savings of the founder (approximately 45 percent), loans and savings (approximately 30 percent), partners, friends, and family (approximately 10 percent), formal venture capital (approximately 10 percent), public offerings and other funding (approximately 5 percent).

The simple availability of risk capital is not enough. Venture capitalists provide directions from the start-up moment to the point where the successful firm can go public. This management advice takes various forms. First, venture capitalists judge, amongst the numerous propositions that they receive, those that offer the best growth potential. This initial selection role is critical. Second, they help entrepreneurs focus on high-growth market opportunities. Third, venture capitalists help crystallize the often incomplete but, technically brilliant, ideas of entrepreneurs. Finally, they identify and attract the key additional players for the entrepreneurial team. The majority of deals financed by venture capitalists require continued attention for periods of five years or more. The real venture capitalist remains committed to his investment for the whole period and is ready to get involved in difficult and unpleasant circumstances when warranted.

Venture capitalists provide "smart money," that is, money with friendly, and at times, imperative advice. Once the new firm is established, managerial advice from personal or professional venture capitalists can become extremely important to its survival. The real venture capitalist, whether acting alone or as part of a professional firm, is the one who supports a start-up in times of difficulty. In fact, venture capitalists spend a substantial proportion of their time attending to budding firms that do not fail but have continued difficulties.

The history of modern venture capital began in the period after World War II. Yet, in New England venturing in technology was active in the eighteenth and early nineteenth centuries as merchants shifted from trade to investment in production. The availability of venture capital from formal and informal sources is a major explanatory factor of the emergence of a high-technology industry in New England in the past forty years.

Venture capitalists are entrepreneurs themselves who gained their experience in other venture capital firms or as technical entrepreneurs. In addition to the funds they provide, the key contributions of venture capitalists are business advice to start-ups in the formative stage and participation in key strategic decisions in the early growth period.

Sources of Venture Capital

Private Investors. Private individual investors, successful entrepreneurs themselves, are a major source of initial financing and advice to technical entrepreneurs. Their knowledge of industry dynamism and their contacts in informal communication networks make it easy to identify and support technical entrepreneurs. Enjoyment, social responsibility, and application of expertise are their main motives.

Entrepreneurs who have been turned down by banks, government programs, and professional venture capital firms can still turn to the informal investor. Due to his role as the last source of financing, the informal investor is often referred to as the individual "crapshooter." But he is not. He usually takes the time to understand a proposal and to diminish the uncertainties that make the venture a high-risk proposal. In reality, informal investors are "guardian angels." They are experienced individuals, with time, money, and a strong motivation to participate in a venture. Given their past entrepreneurial experience, informal investors are often in a good position to work with technical entrepreneurs.

Most informal investors are loners, preferring to work independently rather than tied to the corporate world. By participating actively in the emerging company's board, they have the patience to endure when problems arise. Consequently, individual investors can get involved early in the venture, in the high-risk, high-return phase that characterizes the launching of the start-up. There are other reasons why informal investors are likely to get involved at the early stages of a company's growth: the stakes are usually lower in the early phases, and the individual venture capitalist may not have enough money to get involved in the later rounds of financing.

The process that stimulates individual venture capitalists to spring up is difficult to measure. No statistics are kept about the vast majority of these individuals, as they act alone. Only when they succeed on a grand scale do their cases come out into the open. The available evidence suggests that many do not achieve the returns of the professional venture capital firms, because they are also interested in nonfinancial rewards.

Professional Venture Capitalists. The professional venture capitalist often operates in limited partnerships, acting as a general partner investing the funds of limited partners. Private independent venture capital firms are usually composed of four to eight persons with proven entrepreneurial experience. Private firms act as full-time general managers providing the hands-on monitoring of small portfolios of firms.

These firms do not grow large, mainly because one individual "partner" cannot oversee more than a limited number of investments. Thus, the only way venture capital firms can grow is to aim at bigger deals or to add partners. Bigger deals are also chased by corporations and by underwriters, and competition is tough. Adding partners is easier said than done. In fact, venture capital firms tend to remain small because the best partners often leave when the firms get too big. There is no barrier to entry to talented individuals in this industry.

The professional venture capital industry is heavily concentrated in metropolitan regions such as San Francisco, Boston, London, Houston, Toronto, and Minneapolis. Professional managers in venture firms invest funds supplied by financial institutions, corporations, pension funds, individuals, foundations, and foreign investors.

Professional venture capital firms typically make their investments after the very risky start-up period is over. They leave the start-up phase to the sophisticated individual investors. In general, the majority of investments are made at the early growth stage. Professional investors are very careful in scrutinizing their investment prospects. In fact only 2 out of every 100 opportunities are seriously considered. Furthermore, they seek large commercial return in the near future (five to ten years). The professional venture capitalists will support their investment through the various rounds of financing until such point that it is ready to go public.

Corporate Venture Capital. Corporate venture capital is established by large firms, not only to achieve high returns but to maintain "windows" on emerging technologies and to exploit new product opportunities. In fact, industrial corporations set up venture capital subsidiaries mainly to support their diversification strategies. In particular, corporations fund small ventures with the intention of acquiring the company at a future date.

Corporate venture capital divisions are often modeled after private venture capital firms. They are small clannish "divisions" with a lot of autonomy. Managers are paid on performance, and bonuses can be high. Yet, they have not been able to achieve the same results as professional venture capitalists. The objectives of technical entrepreneurs and those of corporate venture capitalists are often in conflict. For instance, Exxon had set up a venture division as part of its diversification strategy, in the hope of getting into the very profitable information systems business. Within two years, more than half the entrepreneurs left, claiming that they were just unable to get along with the people at Exxon. Nevertheless, corporate successes with venture capital investments abound, especially when limited partnerships with a private venture capital firm have been formed. They should become an increasing source of venture capital.

Government-related Funds. Another source is government-owned or government-supported vehicles, such as Small Business Investment Companies (SBIC). These are generally not as successful as private firms, for they cannot always attract the highly qualified venture professionals. A highly qualified venture capitalist can always start his own firm or join an already established firm. Money is readily available to the smart venture capitalist, without any government intervention. Thus, government schemes to channel funds to venture capitalists usually benefit, not the top-tier venture capitalists who are flooded with partnership proposals, but the "second best" ones. Hence, the generally inferior performance of these publicly supported institutions is explained.

The SBIC was formed subsequent to the enactment of the Small Business Investment Companies Act in 1958. An SBIC is a privately funded firm that can leverage its equity with government-guaranteed loans. A new type of government supported venture capital exists. Business Development Corporations (BDC) have recently emerged. BDCs are public firms that manage money provided by investors who get special tax concessions. In many ways, BDC activities are similar to mutual funds.

Initial public offerings of stock (IPOs) represent a small fraction of the initial financing for high-technology start-ups. Even in the period where "penny stocks" were issued for high-technology start-ups, public offerings did not account for much of the initial financing. Yet, the existence of an active securities market is attractive to technical entrepreneurs and venture capitalists. Investors are interested in start-ups and growth firms with the intention of eventually going public and selling their shares at desirable price–earnings ratios and values. The willingness of investors to acquire public issues of high-technology firms creates conditions whereby venture capitalists can capitalize on the potential of their firms.

Regional Dimensions of Venture Capital

Venture capital is a very local activity, with most venture capitalists investing in the region in which they are located, particularly those who provide start-up financing. It is usually said that a good venture capitalist is not the lead investor in a firm located more than one hour's driving time from his office. Thus, the returns venture capitalists earn are strongly affected by the number of other venture capitalists in that region. They compete amongst themselves for a limited number of investment opportunities with high potential. How, then, has this competition affected the regional performance of the venture capital industry as a whole?

Too many venture capitalists in a region can cause lower returns. But a minimum of venture capitalists in a region is desirable, as venture capitalists often make joint investments and share information. Thus, in many regions and communities, venture capital-availability is inadequate to promote high-growth opportunities. Information networks are not sophisticated enough. Few venture capitalists or wealthy individuals are alerted to the existence of potential high-growth investments. Consequently these regional investors go the conservative route and invest their money in stocks and bonds. The challenge facing regional leaders and public officials is to ensure that there is a sufficient allocation of venture capital within their region to ensure the full exploitation of its potential.

Many regions possess the necessary capital base for the full exploitation of new opportunities. The problem is often an inefficient transfer of information between people with money and entrepreneurs. Regional networks for financial entrepreneurs concerned with high-technology ventures can be developed. Trade fairs and conferences will help to coordinate investors with potential venture investments. Tax incentives can be used to encourage those with money to invest in the venture-capital market. However, the tax benefits should be made to appeal to the individual investors and not to the professional venture capitalists, as good professional venture capitalists are seldom short of funds to invest.

Technical Inputs

No high-technology cluster emerged without the impelling force of several locally owned firms at the leading edge of technology. The founders of these firms were usually graduates of nearby universities, and typically these universities were also at the forefront of technology in various areas. Technical and scientific knowledge on which new venture activities can be based is not a sufficient, but it is a necessary, condition. In other words, without the active role played by corporate or individual entrepreneurs in harvesting state-of-the-art knowledge, technology remains a passive input. The availability of state-of-the-art research activities in a region will make it possible for entrepreneurs to uncover market opportunities.

Networks of Research Organizations

At a very abstract level, technical knowledge and fundamental science are universal and available to potential users across organizations or borders. In reality, learning of scientific and market possibilities is a process that requires intimate experience with on-going research projects funded adequately over a period of years. Individuals involved in research organizations have an opportunity to become aware of state-of-the-art technology and potential market needs. Technology and scientific knowledge are produced by R&D activities in universities, government research institutes, and corporate laboratories. Yet, all research organizations are not equal. Some will never yield state-of-the-art technologies.

Thus, the presence of R&D activity within a region is not enough to develop a high-technology cluster. That the research is performed in market-driven settings and in fruitful scientific fields is what counts. The research network in a region has three functions. First, it keeps pushing the technical frontiers by scientific activities that are related to market needs. Second, it provides would-be technical entrepreneurs with intimate hands-on experience in state-of-the-art technology. Finally, it provides a flow of highly qualified and highly motivated people. Research activities that lead to the technical inputs available to would-be entrepreneurs may be conducted in: the laboratories of established technology-based firms, contract research enterprises, technical universities, and government laboratories.

Market-Driven Research. The advanced laboratories of technology-based firms are prime incubators of high-technology entrepreneurs. Research projects conducted in these laboratories are generally focused on market needs. While the correlation between R&D expenditures and the pursuit of advanced work in laboratories is not perfect, it is clear that an agglomeration of research activities in a region will initiate potential entrepreneurs to technical opportunities.

Contract Research Laboratories. Contract research organizations undertake projects for private firms and government agencies. The idea that useful results for industry could accrue from an organized approach to scientific research leads not only to internal R&D laboratories but also to a contract research business. Amongst leading private contract research firms are Arthur D. Little in Massachusetts, the Batelle Memorial Institute in Ohio, and SRI in California. In Europe, contract research has often been conducted on a cooperative basis through organizations such as in the Centre National de Recherche Métallurgique (CNRM) in Belgium, where steel firms and public authorities joined together to support an industry-oriented research center.

Universities. The emergence of high-technology firms around high-quality technical universities is a well-known phenomenon. Yet, few universities are sources of start-ups. It is not the presence of university laboratories that matters, but the university's commitment to leading-edge research with a view toward industrial applications. Some universities are clearly more oriented to applied work than others.

In fact, only a few universities qualify. The attitude-set fostered in these universities is characterized by close relationships with industrial firms through seminars, contract research, and executive involvement. Students are encouraged to get involved in entrepreneurial activities in which technology is applied to market opportunities. Faculty dependence on contract research stimulates their entrepreneurial drive. Finally, faculty consulting is encouraged to ensure that researchers visualize the market relevance of their activities.

Universities in which professors are working on contract research for government, industrial consortia, or private firms may also be at the origin of the technical knowledge on which new businesses can be based. However, as a general rule, university laboratories, with the exception of contract research institutes, do not usually expose staff intimately to emerging market opportunities or even specialized niches and thin market segments. Spin-offs from technical universities have been common around MIT, but this is an exceptional situation. In fact, a closer examination of spin-offs related to MIT reveals that most are created by graduates involved in contract research institutes and not by university professors. Potential technical ideas abound, but the entrepreneurial spirit must be there, too.

The funding of research activities in universities is highly dependent on government financing, especially in basic research. As time passes, it appears that the funding of basic research by the federal government is an important but indirect factor for technology development. However, basic research is oriented by needs other than market opportunities. In the United States, basic research has been funded by various federal institutions such as the National Science Foundation, the National Institutes of Health, and the Department of Defense. Applied research programs are also financed by those institutions. State governments are taking a more active role in financing applied research institutes in universities that transfer technology to new and existing businesses.

Government Laboratories. Government laboratories are less productive on the entrepreneurial front, because they are often involved in research and development activities not dictated by market needs. The transfer of technology from government laboratories is, therefore, problematic. Few spin-offs emerge directly from such laboratories, especially when they do not subcontract any of their research projects. To improve their connectedness with market needs, some agencies award contracts to research firms or engage in joint research projects with existing technology-based firms.

A large concentration of government sponsored service industry laboratories has been established between Oxford and Wantage in West Berkshire, England. In spite of the presence of more than 20,000 Ph.D.'s in various scientific disciplines, the rate of start-ups of new firms has been very low. Indeed, high technology firms that exist mostly serve the local market, as service firms.

Technical Expertise

Beyond the conduct of R&D activities in market-driven settings lies the market applications potential of the technical areas on which inquiry is focused. At any moment in time, there are "scientific fields" that are fruitful, others that are not. The scientific literature refers to these as "technical trajectories" or "scientific paradigms." Some fields remain productive over many years, others do not. Thus a key element of the infrastructure is the breadth of research activities in technologically potent fields.

As an example of a technical trajectory, one could take microelectronics. The field of microelectronics is certainly appropriate to illustrate the process of evolution of a trajectory. For most, the growth of microelectronics as we know it today, can be traced back to the development of the semiconductor. It is the semiconductor that replaced the thermionic valve which, in turn, allowed for the introduction of new products and components, ranging from mini and microcomputers to electronic games, electronic telecommunications equipment, numerical controls for machine tools, digital watches, and TV remote controls. But the development of the semiconductor does not fully explain the origin of the microelectronics field. In fact, one could trace the origins of this field even further back to the development of the technologies that created the semiconductor industry. There is the development of the first transistor in 1948, made possible through the efforts of Shockley, Bardeen, and Brattain at Bell Laboratories. This led the way to the development of the integrated circuit by Texas Instruments and Fairchild in 1961. In turn, the refinement of the integrated circuit set the stage for the development, in 1971, of the microprocessor which summarizes all the logical functions of a complete computer on a single chip, a far cry from the capacity of the original transistor.

The breadth of the scientific paradigms on which research laboratories work in a particular region will influence the quality and the potency of the technical inputs available to technical entrepreneurs. In some metropolitan regions, a substantial proportion of the research activity is concentrated in a few technical fields in industrial and university laboratories. Some regions develop as "innovation centers" concentrated in fields like pharmaceutical, biomedical, or advanced manufacturing applications. However, metropolitan regions best positioned to profit from the growth potential of many technical trajectories are those in which the portfolio of research activities is composed of a wide array of scientific fields. This is said to be a major advantage of the Boston area.

The funding of research at the early stage of a scientific field has been, in the last fifty years or so, linked with public or military expenditures and the presence of universities. Getting funding to maintain leading-edge research in potentially fruitful trajectories depends on varied types of funding: federal basic or applied scientific research, state expenditure for education, and grants and contract research with industrial partners.

Social Inputs

The development of a high-technology cluster in a region is a slow process that cannot be artificially triggered by political decisions or "quick fix" solutions. Building the institutional conditions that lead to the local initiation of technical ventures is a social process that spreads over many decades. Building high-technology industries in a region requires a long, persistent, and coherent partnership between the private sector, government, and universities.

Analysis of the innovation process, especially in high-technology industries, indicates that a large number of institutional actors are involved over time. An industry rarely emerges due to a sudden breakthrough by a single firm. On the contrary, many institutions are involved. In the case of high-technology industries, participants include universities and their laboratories, advanced research laboratories of private firms, government contracting and procurement agencies, existing high-technology firms, and venture capital suppliers.

Commitment to Progress

A regional commitment to progress is not the fruit of a sudden realization that high technology is important, but the result of a long-standing consensus amongst a region's leadership as to what conditions lead to the emergence of high-technology activities. The process of creating new firms presupposes prior commitments and actions by leaders of key institutions, both in public and private positions. Leaders in the business and university communities can establish, over the years, the institutional foundations for high technology.

High-technology clusters develop in regions where positive attitudes toward the virtues of technology and its contribution to economic growth are widely shared. This mind-set is accepted by both private and public leadership to build the institutions and maintain the activities that convey a commitment to high technology. Such institutional factors are modifiable only over the long run and thus require a long-lasting regional consensus. A commitment to high technology is characterized by a consensus amongst business, banking, academic, and government leaders that fosters continued experimentation, the awarding of initial research and procurement contracts, and the development of high-quality research universities.

The involvement of the private sector in helping to develop the infrastructure is noticeable in many areas. The banking and industrial communities were key partners in the founding of MIT at the end of the nineteenth century. Today, high-technology business leaders still communicate to Boston and Cambridge universities their expected scientific personnel needs. Industry leaders in the Boston area are concerned that the capping of MIT's growth will limit the availability of highly qualified staff and the development of scientific trajectories. They are, therefore, hoping to develop another MIT-type institution in the Boston area. In a similar fashion, the success of Institut Merieux located in Lyons, France, in human and animal vaccines after World War II resulted from a strong commitment by the local business and public leaders: during the same time the publicly funded Institut Pasteur stagnated, though many technical discoveries were made. Similarly, on the West Coast of the United States, the purchase of land for eventual high-technology firms around Stanford University dates back to the early 1930s. A consensus between some university leaders, bankers, and managers of technology-based firms led to the formation of SRI and the development of contract research between Stanford and numerous corporations.

Another key factor for the emergence of a high-technology sector is the existence of a climate that encourages, recognizes, and rewards entrepreneurship. The early years of a start-up are difficult. Without social rewards for their active contribution to economic development, entrepreneurs may be tempted to abandon their ventures for the security of salaried employment. One of the most critical barriers to the emergence of high-technology firms in a region is often social indifference towards technical entrepreneurs. Encouragement and recognition by the local intellectual, financial, and business communities as well as by the media are hard to get when skepticism is common.

Factors that also make a region attractive include the presence of schools and universities, the cost of living, and the quality of life. The taxation structure is another determinant of the climate for entrepreneurship. High individual and corporate income taxes act as deterrents. But these are less important than the general attitudes toward economic development, technology, and entrepreneurial initiatives.

Public Incentives

One can think of public policies that improve the environment for entrepreneurs. For instance, the government plays a critical role in providing contracts for research or a first market for start-up firms. Small high-technology firms start as government contractors or as suppliers to the defense or space market. Some start-ups then shift towards the commercial market. For many high-technology industries such as electronics, aerospace, or nuclear steam systems, research and military contracts played a major developmental role during their critical phases.

Government support of high-technology firms occurs through numerous means: direct procurement of products, equipment, or services; direct support for R&D in firms; support of research in university-related laboratories; and support for initial process or product development. R&D contracts awarded to established firms increase the performance and reliability of products but also give technical entrepreneurs hands-on experience in technology and market windows. Direct purchases, unsolicited proposals, and research contracts serve as a basis to assist the entry of new firms. Defense procurement and support for R&D enhance the mobility of technical entrepreneurs and highly skilled personnel, especially from large to small firms or new ventures.

Diversity in the Industrial and Commercial Base of the Region

The industrial and commercial base of a region is both a cause and a beneficiary of business creation in the high-technology sector. A diversified and rich industrial base will lead to a high rate of business formation and consequently to a rejuvenation of this base. By contrast, a weak industrial and commercial base will lead to few business formations. Positive feedback loops are thus in operation.

A metropolitan agglomeration composed of many growing high-technology firms provides incubation possibilities and initial contracts. An agglomeration of firms in the innovation, rather than maturity, stage is probably the most critical structural factor. In other words, today's industrial structure in a region affects the emergence of high technology.

Innovative and stimulative firms play a developmental role not only by offering market opportunities but also by incubating would-be entrepreneurs. Incubator organizations give potential entrepreneurs the experience necessary to become cognizant of state-of-the-art technology in their fields and to become aware of market opportunities. Technical universities, advanced laboratories, and high-technology firms may be such incubators.

The growth potential of a region and its ability to generate new high-technology activities vary according to the breakdown of firms at maturity, growth, or innovation phases, as well as their shares in the industry in which they operate. Figure 5–1 shows the types of firms in the diverse industrial sectors in a major North American agglomeration.

An agglomeration of effervescent high-technology firms provides attractive work opportunities and incubation possibilities. An agglomeration of such firms also provides thin specialized markets, which create opportunities for locally oriented high-technology firms. These in return, enhance subcontracting possibilities within the pool of specialized staff. Firms entering a growth stage with marketing-intensive strategies also provide opportunities for start-ups in the supply of components.

An agglomeration of technology-based manufacturing and metropolitan service firms will open numerous opportunities for technical entrepreneurs in areas such as services, subcontracting, consulting, or highly specialized niches. Industrial agglomeration makes possible a number of interactions among firms that are highly conducive to innovation. Changing needs for specialized skills can be identified by entrepreneurs or managers of existing firms and rapidly met by the establishment of new firms or internal ventures. The flow of persons from established firms to new firms also acts as a technology transfer mechanism.

A region with a dominance of diversified industrial firms may be high in economic efficiency but low in innovation potential and ability to adapt over time. Firms that have attained the maturity stage where cost efficiency in production and distribution is a chief competitive weapon are not usually good stimulators of high-technology activities. Firms in mature or declining industries are less likely to lead to start-ups and do not provide employees with the technical expertise and the exposure to market opportunities. By contrast, a region may be losing jobs in maturing industries but have emergent sectors that make for the creation of jobs in innovation-related activities. New England, for instance, has retained approximately a substantial share of total employment in the U.S. computer industry in spite of the continual transfer of jobs to lower cost areas.

Sector / Attribute of firms	Effervescent high technology	Mature high technology	Mature manufacturing	Local technical services
Entrepreneurial				
• firms	9 %	2 %	5 %	14 %
• employment	5 %	1 %	8 %	6 %
• example	biotechnology entrant	supercomputer manufacturer	cost leader in equipment manufacturing	PCB layout firm
Growing				
• firms	1 %	6 %	15 %	28 %
• employment	5 %	12 %	35 %	13 %
• example	software product company	manufacturer of mainframe computers	defense and aerospace contractor	software consulting firm
Declining or dormant				
• firms	N/A	2 %	5 %	13 %
• employment		2 %	7 %	6 %
• example		computer manufacturer losing market share	declining car manufacturer	"the boss is old"

Figure 5–1. A Hypothetical Distribution of Firms and Employment

Ossification: The Limits to High-Technology Clusters

The world is full of high-technology clusters past their prime. The process ceased to be self sustaining because of weaknesses in the infrastructure, or it was stopped by internal or external constraints. The clustering process resulting from start-ups and ventures can be accelerated, stopped, and ossified. Whether such events occur will depend on the conditions created in the milieu or as a result of declining external markets for leading high technology industries.

A visit to cities like Glasgow in Scotland, and Pittsburgh and Dayton in the Rustbelt, shows vividly that once upon a time these metropolitan areas were hosts to growing technical industries. This is clearly shown by the factories, the commercial buildings, and the architecture. In other cities the process of growth has led to the dominant position of an industry with few major employers. Cities that come to mind are Detroit with the automobile industry or Rochester with photography and xerography.

The causes of ossification are numerous. The aging of incubators because of market difficulties, the weakening of their leadership, and the focus on maturing industries are major causes of the ossification of a technology cluster. Most corporations age technologically. For instance, fear exists that Control Data Corporation in the Twin Cities, once a leading incubator organization, is no longer as effective in producing start-ups and internal ventures as it once was. The dominance of a few firms and the dependence of numerous high-technology firms as subcontractors on them can be disastrous in a region if these firms slowly ossify.

The lack of foresight in the established business and civic leadership can also lead to the inability to develop new businesses in emerging sectors, such as biomedical, software, or advanced manufacturing. These promising technologies may be lost because the region has not built the required diversity of research activities to compensate for the decline of computer or integrated circuits. Here are three examples of formerly active high-technology clusters.

Dayton

Many Midwest metropolitan cities show vestiges of late nineteenth and early twentieth century high-technology activities. Some suggest that the economic decline has been the result of government policy to channel public funds elsewhere. Whatever the case, many Midwest cities have lost the dynamism they exhibited decades ago. Dayton, Ohio is an example of a once promising technology center that suffered from a lack of investment. The fact that Dayton is home to NCR, IBM, Continental Data Systems, and numerous machine tool companies has been overshadowed by the concurrent wearing out of many major industrial facilities built in the late 1920s.

St. Louis

St. Louis is another city that suffered from a lack of foresight in adapting to changing technology. In the early 1900s St. Louis was a major industrial center, but by World War II, it began to suffer the effects of technological and product obsolescence: companies that had once provided a diversified employment base started to leave, and the auto assembly and the aeronautics industry became dominant. By 1972, 40 percent of St. Louis's manufacturing employment was in aerospace companies. The region came to depend heavily on aerospace, more particularly, on McDonnell-Douglas.

Rochester

At the turn of the twentieth century, the Rochester economy was booming. The city was full of small technology-based firms, and the city promised to be one of the great North American metropolitan areas. Today the city's status and prospects have been greatly reduced to little more than a company town whose character, appearance, and economic health are largely determined by the fate of a few companies. As Eastman-Kodak grew, corporate policies strongly discouraged the spin-off process. Legal action was taken against entrepreneurs who left Kodak to start new firms. Suppliers and the service economy began to serve exclusively Kodak. Small firms were driven out.

Policy Implications

The policy implications that can be drawn from this analysis of the processes and the basic structural conditions that lead to emergence of new technical activities need not lead to simple, "quick-fix" solutions. Economic development with an emphasis on locally initiated high-technology activities will hinge on a long-term commitment. Policy makers in a region need to understand the structure and dynamics of economic development through high technology to plan effective moves. Rhetorical and directive public strategies that disregard the building of an infrastructure for high technology are bound to fail.

Part III
Two Cases of Economic Development Through High Technology

Two case histories of economic development through high technology will be studied to illustrate the conceptual framework outlined in part II. The history and current situation of the high-technology clusters in Minneapolis/St. Paul and Philadelphia will be analyzed in some degree of detail.

The choice of Minneapolis/St. Paul was based on our desire to know the origin and development of a mid-size high-technology cluster that had achieved remarkable successes in mainframe computers, supercomputers, and biomedical technologies. The data on the history and background of the present situation was gathered in Minneapolis/St. Paul through interviews, focus groups, and analysis of published information. The authors are grateful to Hebert G. Johnson, chairman of the Minnesota High-Technology Council, and Charles M. Denny, chairman of both ADC Telecommunications and the Minnesota Technology Corridor Corporation. The impressive characteristics of Minnesota's high-technology cluster are the intense and active commitment to its continued progress that business executives and the public display.

The Philadelphia case was selected because of the role that high technology could play in the revitalization of a large industrial agglomeration that suffered severe economic losses during the 1960s and early 1970s. The case of the Philadelphia cluster was developed through personal interviews and analyses of published data. The authors wish to express their thanks to Lee Stull, director of the Greater Philadelphia International Network, and John D'Aprix, president of the University City Science Center.

Our first discovery in analyzing the Philadelphia situation was the visual presence of many high-technology firms around Philadelphia along Highway 202. Many real-estate developers were active because they perceived an acceleration in the rate of high-technology business formation and the migration of high-technology firms toward suburban locations. Modest progress in the high-technology sector had the effect of developing positive attitudes and a sense that even greater achievements were possible.

6
The Minnesota High-Technology Cluster: Origin and Present Situation

The Twin Cities area is home to a fairly dynamic high-technology cluster, with over 1,600 firms employing approximately 150,000 persons in 1987. Among American metropolitan areas, the Twin Cities' high-technology cluster ranks as a mid-size but relatively fast growing area, especially in terms of the number of new establishments. The Twin Cities' high-technology cluster ranks seventeenth in the United States insofar as the number of high-tech establishments is concerned. It ranks fifteenth in the growth of new establishments, with a net gain of 661 new firms between 1971 and 1984. It ranks twenty-second in terms of growth of employment, with a net gain of more than 25,000 jobs from 1971 to 1984.

A Home-Grown Cluster

The Minneapolis/St. Paul high-technology cluster is basically home grown. Less than 9 percent of establishments are owned by out-of-state firms. Approximately half of the establishments owned by out-of-state corporations were home grown but later acquired.

The vast majority of the 1,600 firms that form the Minnesota high-technology cluster in 1987 employ less than 100 persons. Only 175 high-technology firms have more than 100 employees. The orientations of high-technology firms in the Minnesota high-technology cluster are regional, national, and international in scope. Table 6–1 gives a distribution of firms according to their market orientation.

The Twin Cities constitute the manufacturing core of Minnesota, and over a third of that manufacturing falls into the high-technology category. Yet the vast majority of high-technology firms are service oriented. Approximately 45 percent are involved in services, 15 percent in distribution of high-technology products, and the remaining 40 percent in manufacturing and sales.

Table 6–1
Distribution of Market Orientation of
Minnesota's High-Technology Firms, 1986

Regional orientation only	41.0%
National orientation only	8.5
International orientation only	3.0
Regional and national orientation	22.0
Regional, national and international orientation	25.5
Total	100.0

Table 6–2
Types of Customers of Minnesota High-
Technology Firms, 1986

Individual consumers	17.2%
Other high technology firms	19.8
Industrial and commercial firms	29.6
Governmental agencies	13.7
Educational institutions	5.6
Foreign firms	2.4
Medical institutions	7.0
Others	4.7
Total	100.0

The customers of high-technology firms range from individual con-
sumers to other high-technology firms and general industry and governmen-
tal units. Table 6–2 displays a breakdown of types of customers of high-
technology firms in the Twin Cities area.

The Emergence of the Minnesota
High-Technology Agglomeration

In the late 1940s, Minnesota's economy was heavily oriented towards farming, food processing, mining, and manufacturing. Not many could foresee
that an agglomeration of high-technology firms would one day develop. The
traditions of hard work and entrepreneurship in Minnesota, as well as the

active involvement of informal venture capital and established corporations, have made it possible to grow a high-technology cluster from five major wellsprings in the immediate post–World War II years.

The five major initial incubators were: Engineering Research Associates, General Mill's mechanical division, the Rosemount Research Laboratory, the medical school and hospitals of the University of Minnesota, and 3M.

During World War II, the Rosemount Research Laboratory, at the University of Minnesota, was engaged in explosive and ballistic research. At the end of the war, Dr. Ackerman, its director, turned the installation into a center for supersonic research. Many spin-offs emerged from this contract research organization, namely, Rosemount Engineering, Fluidyne, and MTS. Also during the war effort, the mechanical division of General Mills engaged in research and manufacturing activities that led to numerous advances in manufacturing technology and numerical controls.

The fortuitous move of a group of engineers to St. Paul and the formation of Engineering Research Associates (ERA) was to have a lasting impact on the development of high technology in Minnesota. ERA's origins comprise a World War II classified Navy unit called "Communications Supplementary Activities—Washington" (CSAW). CSAW was a collection of cryptologists, mathematicians, engineers, and physicists deciphering Axis codes, intercepting high-frequency radio transmissions, and pinpointing the movements of enemy ships. These tasks required the use of computing devices. The CSAW also investigated electronic solutions to cryptologic problems. The group was coordinated by several supervisors, among them Commander Howard T. Engstrom and Lt. Commander William C. Norris, As World War II ended, plans to establish a private company were formed by Engstrom, Norris, and Captain Ralph I. Meader with John E. Parker, an investment banker in Washington, D.C. During World War II, Parker headed Northwestern Aeronautical Corporation (NAC) in St. Paul. In January 1946, a new company, Engineering Research Associates, Inc. was incorporated, and it located in the Twin Cities because facilities were available. An investment group led by Parker owned 50 percent; the technical group headed by Engstrom, Norris, and Meader owned the other half.

ERA was purchased in 1952 by Remington Rand, which merged with the Sperry Corporation in 1955. The Sperry Univac division was established to manufacture computers and peripheral equipment. Several spin-offs from this division occurred in the late 1950s and early 1960s. Figure 3–3 shows the major entities derived from Sperry Rand and Control Data, its major spin-off in 1957.

The University of Minnesota's medical school emphasized clinical research and received federal funding for the development of a world-class research network. In the 1950s, research activities at the University of Minnesota's medical school, St. Jude Hospital, and the Mayo Clinic in Rochester, generated spin-offs that subsequently became leading incubators themselves. Some of these include Medtronics, Angiomedics, CP, and CPM .

The biomedical industry grew around Medtronics Inc. and the University of Minnesota's surgery research programs. Cooperative efforts between Dr. C. Walton Lillehei and Earl Bakken, cofounder of Medtronics Inc., made possible the development of the first cardiac pacemaker in 1958. Since 1949, when Medtronics was established, many companies producing medical devices have been founded in Minnesota. Spin-offs emerged from established firms and from biomedical research at the University of Minnesota. Spin-offs from Medtronics include: Cardiac Pacemakers Inc., Renal Systems, Stimulation Technology, EMPI, Aequitron Medical, Med Tel, Medical Devices Inc., Pharmadyne Corp., Vivatron Inc., WR Medical Electronics Company, Population Research, Angiocor, Biomedicus Inc., Sci Med Life Systems, and Mentor.

The story of 3M does not need to be told. Its reputation as an innovative and entrepreneural corporation was built on its ability to start new ventures internally. 3M has contributed to the development of the Twin Cities high-technology cluster mainly through internal corporate projects.

The present annual rate of business creation is relatively high in the Twin Cities, with between 100 and 125 high-technology start-ups annually. Approximately 25 to 30 start-ups and expansions are financed by the formal venture capital industry. Most start-ups are financed by independent venture capitalists or by entrepreneurs themselves. The annual rate of business addition in the last ten years has been, on average, 90 firms per year. Two sectors, biomedical and software, each account for 25 percent of this growth.

Incubation and entrepreneurial spin-offs led to two waves of business formation in the 1950s and 1960s and again in the 1980s. The first wave was linked to computers and electronics while the second wave is heavily focused in the biomedical, biotechnology, and software fields.

A large number of start-ups have been created in the last five years. First, numerous software enterprises supporting existing firms have been established. Only a few have experienced sustained growth. The electronics sector has also sustained many start-ups: Computer Network Technology, Metatek, Digigraphic Systems, Infinite Graphics, Pattern Processing Technologies, Xtal Corp., UTC, Magnetic Data, King Computer Systems, Technology 8-0, Hinland Electronics, Applied Vision Systems, and Cyberoptis. The biomedical field has also experienced a rapid rate of business creation with Angicor, Angiomedics, GV Medical, Biovascular, Eye Technology, Implant Technologies, STI, and AVI. Local start-ups in the telecommunications field in the last five years include Applied Spectrum, Network Communications, and Republic Telecommunications. Finally, in the supercomputer sector, recent start-ups include Edge Computers, Zycad, and Star Technologies.

Except for the IBM plant in Rochester and a few subcontractors or stand-alone companies, there has been little branching out of the Twin Cities into the rest of Minnesota.

Processes That Led to the Emergence of a High-Technology Cluster

The growth of the Minnesota high-technology cluster depended in large part on the vitality and dynamism of a self-feeding agglomeration that thrived in the Twin Cities. In other words, the process of new business creation and expansion depended to a great extent on structural factors that were in place as a result of past actions and achievements. Let us examine the major processes that explain the growth of this high-technology cluster.

An Entrepreneurial Tradition

A strong entrepreneurial tradition gave rise to rapid growth of new business formation in the 1950s and 1960s in computers, electronics, and biomedical technologies. The rate of business formation decreased in the 1970s, especially in electronics. A resurgence of new business formation has occurred in the 1980s in the software, electronics, and biomedical fields. In the last five years the sectors in which business creation was high have been data processing and software, professional services, telecommunications, and biomedical technology.

Established firms such as Control Data, 3M, and Medtronics have promoted the entrepreneurial tradition both inside and outside their organizations. Internal corporate programs have been established in many corporations. 3M's internal venturing programs have received wide acclaim. Furthermore, seed capital funds have been established by many corporations. For instance, the Minnesota Seed Capital fund was established by fifteen corporate investors, including such well known names as Control Data Corporation, Data Card Corporation, 3M, and Dayton Hudson Corporation.

A Diversified Technology Base

The diversity of the technological base in the Twin Cities is high, as can be observed in table 6–3. Despite missing out somewhat in the semiconductor and microcomputer technical waves, Minnesota presently leads in the supercomputer and biomedical fields. The only sector feeling a lag in technology is defense and aerospace, which is also the largest high-technology sector in Minnesota in terms of employment.

The extent of technical diversity allows cross fertilizations that become the basis for business development. For example, knowledge and experience

Table 6–3
Number of High-Technology Firms across
Technological Sectors in Minnesota, 1986

Data processing and software	401
Pharmaceuticals and biotechnology	43
Defense and aerospace	17
Communications	50
Manufacturing technologies	88
Biomedical	107
Computers	58
Electronic parts and components	213
R&D	89
Engineering and architecture services	534
Total	1,600

Source: Estimates by Secor from data provided by the Department of Energy and Economic Development of Minnesota.

in electronics and information processors have been used to develop superior biomedical products and instruments used in biotechnology research and control.

Success Stories

Visible and successful start-ups presented role models and further stimulated entrepreneurship. Role models allow entrepreneurs to better understand the uncertainty involved and the strategies that lead to risk reduction in marketing, product development, organization design and financing. The rapid growth of MTS, Medtronics, Cray Research, Edge Computers, and Network Systems proves that entrepreneurship is a viable career path for scientists, engineers, and managers.

The Presence of Corporate Headquarters

The Twin Cities' high-technology cluster is basically home grown and has led over the years to the development of large corporations with headquarters in either Minneapolis or St. Paul. The presence of a large number of corporate headquarters has caused the establishment of numerous research centers in the Twin Cities. Research centers exist at 3M, Control Data, FMC Corp. VTC, Cray Research, Honeywell, ETA Systems, Sperry, UTI, Rosemont Engineering, Medtronics, Angiomedics, CPI, and CPM.

Established corporations play several critical roles in the stimulation of high technology. Internally, to penetrate new markets or exploit technical opportunities, established corporations initiate new product-development projects, allow the initiation of venture projects, or develop new business opportunities that are compatible with their present strategic mission. Externally, established corporate headquarters stimulate the emergence of high-technology firms by innovative and experimental procurement policies directed at small firms, involving supply agreements, strategic alliances, equity investments, and joint ventures.

The Quality of Life in Minnesota

The quality of life in the area is perceived as high by Twin Cities executives. However, Minnesota is not considered a place desirable to which to migrate by the nation's university graduates. Moreover, Minnesota is perceived as a highly taxed state even though recent efforts have been made to lower the tax burden for individuals.

Three factors contribute to the quality of life in the Twin Cities area: Minnesota is felt to be a good place to raise a family, particularly because of the quality of health-care and education services; Minnesota is viewed as a sound moral milieu where traditional values still prevail: and the four distinct seasons are attractive to the outdoors-oriented.

Informal and Formal Venture Capital

Minnesota benefits from a high level of venture capital activity, both through formal venture capital and through informal networks nurtured by a long tradition of involvement. The formal venture capital industry invested $150 million in 1985 ($45 million in 1981), placing Minnesota sixth among all the states. Close to half the investments are made in Minnesota, the rest mainly in the East Coast and in California. The average investment by a venture capital firm was $495,000 in 1984. Almost all (94 percent of the investments in the state occurred in the Twin Cities–metropolitan area.

The venture capital industry in Minnesota is composed not only of private limited partnerships but includes a strong presence by public corporations. A number of leading firms, such as CDC, Honeywell, Medtronic, and Sperry, have established venture capital seed funds to support emerging firms.

The formal venture capital industry is active at the seed and start-up stages where approximately 50 percent of the deals are made. In 1985, of all the deals made in Minnesota, 4.7 percent of the funds were invested in seed operations, 50.4 percent in start-up operations, 41.7 percent in first-stage investments, and 3 percent in second-stage investments. In 1985, 52 percent of all funds were invested in start-up firms, compared with 36 percent in

1986. The cyclical nature of investments in start-up operations indicates the volatile nature of venture-capital investments. As compared to the national venture-capital industry, Minnesota's venture-capital investments are slightly higher on start-ups.

The medical and health-care sectors received the largest share (36 percent in 1985) of the total investment in Minnesota. The medical industry also saw the most significant growth in previous investment years. The computer hardware and software industries rank second as an investment area, with 29 percent of the total share. This represents a decline from the level of 52 percent in 1981. Electronics and advanced manufacturing techniques are high-technology sectors in which investments are also focused.

Individual investors have traditionally played an important role in Minnesota. Direct investments by individuals backing entrepreneurs is still the most common way of funding start-ups in Minnesota. The vast majority of start-ups (85-90 percent) do not receive formal venture capital funding but rely either on the entrepreneurs' own funds or on informal venture capital sources. Many individual investors are part of networks that assist fledgling firms in getting contacts with venture-capital firms for later-stage investments. Moreover, private investors are also active in helping the firms establish useful commercial contacts with well-established firms, leading to contracts as suppliers and subcontractors.

A Strong Public–Private Partnership

The business leadership of the Twin Cities, whether involved in high-technology manufacturing or service industries, has traditionally assumed its "corporate social responsibility" to contribute to the economic development of the area and to the improvement of the quality of life in the Twin Cities-area. The Minnesota Business Partnership, the Minnesota Project on Corporate Responsibility, and the Minnesota High Technology Council are three prime examples of social responsibility in action.

The Minnesota Business Partnership was formed in 1978 as a vehicle for involving corporate chief executives and senior managers in public matters. The Partnership is organized around task forces on such issues as small business, job creation, communications, education, and transportation. These task forces analyze long-range economic issues and work to achieve political consensus among public and private sector groups in addressing these issues. Their work has resulted in a number of specific initiatives relevant to high-technology development.

The Minnesota Cooperation Office (MCO) helps entrepreneurs with the conception, planning, staffing, and financing of their businesses. By harnessing the experience of established entrepreneurs and business executives, MCO supports entrepreneurs in the development and implementation of their business plans. Approximately fifty firms and organizations in the Twin Cities contribute funds and information to MCO.

The Minnesota Seed Capital Fund provides early-stage, start-up financing for firms promising significant job creation. Investments range from $50,000 to $250,000.

Mid-America International Trading was formed in 1981 to assist both small and medium-sized businesses in the Midwest to market their products and services internationally.

Finally with the STARCO, or Help-Start-a-Company Program, each participating company makes a commitment to help start at least one new company through the assignment of a high-level executive to work as an in-house promoter to marshal resources in support of start-up businesses. Investing companies receive equity or royalties.

The Minnesota Project on Corporate Responsibility aims to promote awareness of the changing nature of corporate responsibility by involving corporate executives in the study of examples of responsible actions by United States companies.

The Minnesota High Technology Council, a non-profit organization created in 1982, works to promote an environment conducive to the formation of firms and to the growth of technology-intensive industries. The Council is focusing on the identification of high-technology industries' present and future needs, improvement of the educational system to produce highly qualified personnel and scientists, and the promotion of the awareness of the role played by high technology in economic development. The Minnesota High Technology Council is supported by over 100 firms and has a widespread individual membership.

The Work Ethic in Minnesota

The work ethic of employees and entrepreneurs provided fertile soil for the emerging computer, electronics, and biomedical fields in the 1950s and early 1960s. A consensus exists to the effect that Minnesota's work force is characterized by an unusually strong work ethic and commitment to high-quality products and services.

Some Dangers on the Horizon

One of the major dangers of the Minnesota economic fabric is the aging of its traditional incubators, those large firms that spun off new firms in the past. Many of the successful incubators of the last thirty years operate in industries that are themselves in the process of maturation. This fact is made clear by the rate of business creation, which is higher in biomedical technologies than in the electronics or computer fields.

Many of these firms invest less than they used to in R&D and internal ventures due to financial difficulties. Probably as a result of the aging of many incubators, Minnesota's high-technology industries have performed unevenly in a number of new markets such as semiconductors, microcomputers, and minicomputers.

There are no prime defense and aerospace contractors in the Twin Cities area. Prime contractors play a critical role in the allocation of subcontracts and in the development of prototypes when new technologies are developed and tested. The Twin Cities' defense and aerospace sector is characterized by numerous subcontractors, which have a narrower focus and are often involved in less critical technologies than prime contractors. Moreover, subcontractors generally provide less technical support to their own subcontractors than do prime contractors. It is thus more difficult for Minnesota to be at the leading edge in the defense and aerospace sector.

High technology is a "people" activity that relies on attracting and keeping highly qualified personnel. These persons often tend to select their region of preference when they attend graduate school or immediately thereafter. Later moves are much more costly for an individual. Minnesota has a problem attracting highly qualified, technically oriented, graduate students and professionals from out-of-state. Minnesota is not seen as the best place in North America for an ambitious, technologically oriented person. It faces strong competition from both East and West Coasts and increasingly, from the southern states.

The Business Creation Potential

In preparing this case we examined eight technological areas to assess the future business creation potential. These sectors were biotechnology, electronics, advanced manufacturing technologies, biomedical products, supercomputers, software, defense and aerospace, and telecommunications. Biomedical products and electronics parts and instruments were the two sectors expected to experience the highest rate of new business formation in the coming years. Our ranking of the new business creation potential of the eight technical sectors is shown in table 6–4.

Sectors with the highest present employment are expected to be low contributors to new businesses, as they are mature and because defense expenditures in real terms are expected to remain flat in the future. On the other

Table 6–4
Rankings of Technological Sectors, 1986

	Present Employment	*Business Creation Potential*
Biomedical technologies	1	7
Electronics	2	5
Biotechnology	3	8
Software and data processing	4	4
Telecommunications	4	6
Advanced manufacturing	4	2
Aerospace and defense	7	3
Supercomputers and computers	8	1

hand, several sectors with lower employment, such as biomedical technologies, electronics, and biotechnology are expected to lead in business creation. Let us examine briefly each one of these sectors.

Biomedical Products

The U.S. market for biomedical products is growing at a high rate as a consequence of four basic trends pertaining to both demand and supply. Demographics are changing and the proportion of older persons and disadvantaged people receiving treatment increases. The desire for wellness is widely shared in the population. The technology for delivering drugs is undergoing major changes, thus opening up new opportunities. Greater reliance on free enterprise to develop biomedical products is evident.

Numerous small firms pursuing niches are entering the industry. The presence of large firms is not a major obstacle to entry in this fragmented industry. The biomedical sector in Minnesota is composed mainly of small and medium-sized firms. Minnesota has been a leader in the orientation towards health and the emphasis on wellness. The region has sponsored numerous health innovations such as health maintenance organizations. The high rate of business formation in this field is linked to active research programs at the University of Minnesota. Minnesota as a major medical center has the University hospitals and the Mayo clinic. A large volume of new medical and biomedical knowledge is generated in these institutions and can be transferred to small or large companies for implementation and new product development.

Electronics

The electronics industry is becoming a service industry to other high-technology sectors with different growth potentials. Sectors of high growth are in telecommunications, medical instrumentation, customized integrated circuits, gate arrays, and mini and supercomputers. Entry into electronics is easy, especially in niche markets. However, entry into mass markets or integrated circuit production requires substantial capital investment.

In Minnesota, strong sectors are defense electronics, computers, and in-house semiconductors. During the late 1960s and the 1970s business creation in electronics was low in Minnesota. However, in the 1980s, approximately fifty firms pursuing niches have been established as a result of opportunities arising from the personal computer. The pursuit of niches by new firms and the constant development of new products by established firms will assure the growth of electronics in Minnesota. Opportunities exist in defense, computers, and biomedical products as suppliers of components and parts.

Biotechnology

Biotechnology is a major industry of the future, presently going from research to product sales. In their shift from research to product marketing, firms are facing difficulties associated with FDA regulations and product liabilities. Many firms could fail in this transition.

Biotechnology in Minnesota rests on a dozen entrepreneurial firms, many tracing their origin to the University. A number of success stories, such as Endotronics, are stimulating entrepreneurs in the region. Minnesota ranks fourth in the United States in biotechnology after San Francisco Bay, New England, and San Diego. Federal and state support is vital for the continued growth of biotechnology in Minnesota. Biotechnology is one field in which the social rate of return of research far exceeds the private rate of return.

Software Products and Services

The market for software products is complex and segmented. It will grow mostly in niches for specialized applications. Examples of such niches are applications and interfaces for supercomputers, generic applications for personal computers, content specific applications, and consulting services. Entry into the software industry is easy but marketing skills are necessary to assure the growth of any firm. Because of the existence of multiple niches, the software market is a fertile ground for entrepreneurs. Concentrations exist especially around leading universities where highly specialized faculty members train graduate students who then develop software products.

Opportunities have led to the creation of approximately 1,000 small software firms in Minnesota, many are one-person operations. Few have become large. Computer and supercomputer firms as well as corporate headquarters are seen as major customers for emerging software firms. Supercomputer applications offer opportunities but local companies do not yet emphasize this area.

Advanced Manufacturing Technologies

Good opportunities exist in advanced manufacturing technologies. A world market potential of $38 billion in 1990 is expected, with annual growth of around 20 percent per year, especially in information-related areas. Opportunities abound in some industry applications, discrete-part manufacturing, process control—eventually using supercomputers, manufacturing information management, and computer-automated manufacturing.

The penetration of advanced manufacturing technologies in the United States is not very high. Most companies are still at the stage of understanding their manufacturing processes to improve control, apply expert systems, or establish islands of automation. Cautious manufacturing executives hesitate to leapfrog to computer integrated manufacturing or rely on robotics applications that may fail to deliver performance. Numerous opportunities exist where industry executives, in cooperation with specialized advanced manufacturing firms, take time to plan and implement solutions that focus not only on labor cost reduction but mostly on understanding and integrating total manufacturing cycles.

Minnesota has definite strengths in precision manufacturing electronics and computers. Opportunities can be exploited by established computer, aerospace, and engineering firms, and by alliances between large and smaller firms and small niche firms.

Telecommunications

The telecommunications industry is changing under the influence of both deregulation and new business entrants pursuing opportunities in products and services. The growth of activity in telecommunications is centered around the East Coast, Dallas, Silicon Valley, Los Angeles, Germany, Japan, France, and Sweden. In the last ten years, many start-ups have penetrated the industry as distributors, vendors, and application specialists. The next ten years will be characterized by entries into specialized niches: service to financial institutions, visual telephones, videotexts, and specialized databanks.

Few success stories have emerged in Minnesota in the last five years in telecommunications. A limited number of new firms in Minnesota have established themselves in this sector. Yet, the Minnesota computer industry as well as the experience developed in the electronics industry are two strengths upon which new businesses could be created by entrepreneurs.

Defense and Aerospace

The defense and aerospace boom of the last five years is not expected to continue. Growth will be very small in the next ten years, and it will be accompanied by major shifts in the industry. Nontraditional products and services such as information processing systems, advanced electronic optics, and composite materials will experience growth whereas traditional systems characterized by metal fabrication and hydraulics will decline.

Firms to benefit will be the ones offering products embodying electronics, optics, composite materials, and sensor control. As a consequence, defense and aerospace firms need to commit substantial R&D expenditures to keep aware of technologies that may displace their products.

The industry is dominated by U.S. prime contractors. Minnesota's firms are not prime contractors. Honeywell, Sperry, and FMC are generally subcontractors participating in team bidding with other specialty firms. Even though defense and aerospace is the largest high-technology sector in terms of employment, many Minnesota firms fear lagging behind in the technologies that will be incorporated in new weapons systems. A large number of subcontractors depend on the future of Minnesota's defense and aerospace firms.

Supercomputers

The supercomputer industry was born in the Twin Cities by the spin-off of Cray Research from Control Data. The supercomputer industry with sales projections of up to $1 billion per year is dominated by two Minnesota firms with 70 percent of the world market: Cray Research and ETA Systems. With the entry of Japanese firms and the rise of near supercomputers, mostly in California, no new entries are expected in the industry.

Supercomputer firms are dedicated to building faster machines and thus tend to neglect market opportunities that exist in human-machine interfaces and software applications. Opportunities not exploited by supercomputer firms are: software applications for targeted industries, generic software applications, and software for computer-aided design and imaging, and graphic-human interfaces.

The ability to develop these software applications in Minnesota is a major asset. Yet, entries are not occurring as fast as elsewhere because the perceived market for supercomputer applications is small.

Conclusion

Minnesota stands as a second-tier state, insofar as high technology is concerned. Most high-technologies activities in Minnesota are concentrated in the Twin Cities. High-technology firms in Minnesota are basically home grown, reflecting a high level of entrepreneurial activities. The pillars of the high-technology sector, computer, and biomedical industries are built around local firms started after the war. Minnesota's high-technology sector is also well diversified, with additional strength in electronics, communications, data processing and software, defense, and aerospace. Minnesota also benefits from a strong local venture capital industry. There are weaker points that hinder the growth of high technology in Minnesota. Minnesota's success stories in high technology are now aging. There are no large prime defense contractors. The University of Minnesota, which ranks sixth among U.S. colleges and universities for R&D spending, is in danger of slipping slowly as an R&D powerhouse. And finally, Minnesota does not attract would-be entrepreneurs as easily as the East and West Coast states, because it suffers from an image problem.

7
The Case of the Metropolitan Philadelphia Area

The turnaround in attitudes and the growth of high technology in the metropolitan Philadelphia region will be described. This rejuvenation was made possible by mobilization of the region's business leadership as well as by an increase in the rate of new business creation, both building on the already existing educational and industrial base of the region.

A Period of Decline: The Erosion of the Manufacturing Base

Philadelphia has experienced an erosion of its manufacturing base since World War II. Between 1952 and 1984, the number of jobs in manufacturing in the metropolitan area fell by one-third, down from 595,900 to 396,300. Nevertheless, overall employment in the area increased by one-third during this period, from 1,474,800 to 1,983,700, as growth in the service sector made up for losses in manufacturing employment.

While the population of the United States increased 11 percent between 1970 and 1980, the metropolitan Philadelphia population decreased 2 percent, and the Philadelphia city population diminished by 13 percent. In the 1970s, the metropolitan Philadelphia area lagged behind national employment growth in virtually all generally defined industries. Even areas historically strong in this region's economy, like machinery manufacturing, weakened considerably. During those years, the only areas to increase in Philadelphia were research and scientific equipment manufacturing.

The movement of employment from the Philadelphia region to the rest of the United States is reflected in the region's growth rate relative to that of the United States (1 percent compared with 2 percent between 1952 and 1972, 0.6 percent compared with somewhat less than 2 percent between 1972 and 1983). In short, U.S. growth rates between 1952 and 1983 were two to three times that of the Philadelphia metropolitan region. Two processes were associated with this period of decline: a shift in the industrial structure of the region and decentralization from the urban core to surrounding urban communities.

A Shift in the Industrial Structure

The shift in the industrial structure from a heavy reliance on the manufacturing sector to an increase in the importance of services parallels a similar shift in the United States as table 7–1 indicates. The decline in both total manufacturing and durable goods employment in the Philadelphia region has been long term and persistent.

A revitalization and restructuring of the economy of the Delaware Valley occurred in the first half of the 1980s. The shift in employment in the Philadelphia region, particularly the change from manufacturing to service-producing sectors, is clear. In 1970, 32 percent of Philadelphia's employment was in manufacturing, compared to 27 percent nationally. By 1985, both the United States and the Delaware Valley derived approximately 20 percent of their employment from manufacturing. The nongovernment service-producing sector's local importance grew from 50 percent in 1970 to 62 percent in 1985 as compared to the U.S. average, which increased from 49 percent in 1970 to 58 percent in 1985.

Between 1970 and 1982 total employment in metropolitan Philadelphia grew only 6.2 percent, or 0.5 percent annually. Since 1982, total employment has increased by 5.8 percent or 1.9 percent compared to a national rate of 2 percent in the 1970–1982 period and 2.9 percent since 1982. The employment growth gap between the United States and the Philadelphia region is thus narrowing.

Compared to the nation as a whole, the industrial structure of the Philadelphia metropolitan region contains more firms and employment in faster growing industries than in the slower growing industries. In effect, the local industrial mix lends strength to the argument that the region's restructuring has positioned it to where it could outperform the nation in terms of employment growth. In effect, Philadelphia is becoming more dependent on service sector jobs than many other areas. A similar process occurred in Massachusetts in the early and mid-1970s.

Urban Decentralization

The phenomenon of urban decentralization brought a significant redistribution in employment and population. Between 1970 and 1980, the city of Philadelphia incurred a 13.4 percent decline in population, and the city's share of metropolitan-area population fell from 40.4 percent to 35.5 percent. Over the same period, total employment declined 15.1 percent and the city's share of metropolitan-area employment receded from 51.3 percent to 38.6

Table 7–1
Employment Changes in the Metropolitan Philadelphia Region, 1970–1980

	Philadelphia	SMSA	United States
Total nonagricultural employment	− 15.0%	6.6%	27.9%
Private sector	− 17.3	5.5	27.7
Contract construction	− 38.3	− 8.1	24.6
Manufacturing	− 42.9	− 19.9	5.1
Transportation, communications, and public utilities	− 22.1	− 6.6	14.2
Wholesale and retail trade	− 18.8	− 13.5	36.8
Finance, insurance, and real estate	− 6.6	22.8	41.6
Services	19.2	41.3	54.2
Government	− 4.2	12.9	28.8
Total population	− 13.4	− 2.2	11.5

Source: Summers and Luce: Federal Reserve Bank, Philadelphia, 1986.

percent. In 1986, the city contained only 35.7 percent of the total metropolitan-area employment.

The economy of the city of Philadelphia failed to grow as rapidly as the metropolitan economy because overall rates of job creation in the central city lagged behind those in the metropolitan region while overall rates of job losses in the city exceeded those in the metropolitan region. In the post-1980 period, development in the Philadelphia metropolitan area has been based on growth of existing firms more than other urban areas, or the nation, have. The continued ability of the regional economy to create new jobs through the formation of new enterprises must be seen as a definite strength. Specially in the Route 202 corridor, where over 200 high-technology firms have recently emerged.

At the metropolitan level, only manufacturing employment has suffered an absolute decline in the last ten years. All other sectors of the regional economy registered modest gains. Within the central city, however, all sectors have performed less well than in the metropolitan region at large, with deep losses in manufacturing. Significant growth in employment in the central city was registered only by producers and consumer services.

A Climate of Optimism

In the mid-1980s the metropolitan Philadelphia economy showed strength as unemployment leveled at 6 percent, and the rate of growth of employment outpaced the national average. In the late 1980s an air of confidence is replacing the negative attitudes prevalent in the 1970s. Following several years of sizeable job losses, the manufacturing employment base stabilized.

The increased diversification of economic activity in the Philadelphia region has provided a wider base for economic growth. Many of the new jobs have been created in smaller firms with less than 100 employees and a broader spectrum of economic activity. Reliance on a few very large firms in a limited number of industries has somewhat diminished since the early 1980s.

Over the period from 1971 to 1984, numerous new jobs and firms have been created in the high-technology sector as table 7–2 indicates. Between 1977 and 1982, high-technology sectors grew at a rate exceeding their growth in the nation. While Philadelphia cannot be said to rank among the fastest growing places, it is nonetheless a major center of technology-related industries in the United States. In 1985, nine sectors dominated the employment picture in the Philadelphia area. Three of the nine (computer services and data processing, communications equipment, and pharmaceuticals) contained more than a third of regional high-technology employment. The second group, called large sectors in table 7–2, followed the national pattern more closely than the group of largest sectors.

The growth of high technology in the Philadelphia metropolitan region is such that approximately 30 percent of present manufacturing activities fall into the broad category of advanced technology. By 1986, Philadelphia appears to have closed the growth gap that had existed between it and the rest of the country, largely by maintaining growth during a period when national growth rates were declining.

Accounting for the Modest Turnaround

The turnaround in the Philadelphia area has been accomplished by economic readjustments such as reducing wages to national levels and developing of services sectors, including high technology, by business creations and expansions. Yet, economic adjustment results from business decisions. It is our observation that mobilization of the public and private leadership in the region played a significant role in making this turnaround possible. In fact, the rejuvenation of the Philadelphia metropolitan area was a process that spanned more than a decade of mobilizing community resources and rebuilding communication networks in a city that was basically rich in unused resources.

Mobilization of the Leadership

The shock of losing a substantial part of the traditional manufacturing base has slowly triggered a mobilization of the business leadership in the Philadelphia area. Business and civic leaders, at the sight of dying textile and metal-forming industries, decided to act. The mobilization of the business communities was not instantaneous but took over a decade. H. Perlmutter, a professor at the Wharton School, is credited by many executives as a key initiator of the process. Many attempts and a series of voluntary committees were necessary to get the diverse constituencies together.

The old leadership in Philadelphia is said to be traditional and conservative. Established leaders and bankers were often Philadelphia natives who belonged to a rather closed social circle. During the late 1960s and 1970s, the leadership in banking and manufacturing was slowly modified by an inflow of outsiders and managers who assumed executive positions. Many of the new business leaders were not native Philadelphians but executives who were promoted to chief executive officer (CEO) positions, or real-estate developers who took an active interest in the region.

The Philadelphia Partnership was established in the early 1970s by local business leaders to promote economic development. Business leaders agreed that the city government was not active enough in promoting economic development but instead focused on other issues. A movement of reform of the city administration was initiated within the community.

The emerging business leadership can be described not only as visible and forceful executives getting involved in promoting the region but as a cooperative system of diverse constituencies. For instance, a number of new networks to promote economic development were established by concerned executives: networks of successful entrepreneurs who act as consultants to new firms; networks of informal venture capitalists; and linkages between the Chamber of Commerce, the University City Science Center, and the Greater Philadelphia Economic Development coalitions. Committees were formed to handle the many problems that needed solutions. The committees dealt with issues such as:

Inadequate local venture capital activities

Marketing of the region's potential to corporate executives and entrepreneurs in Philadelphia

Renovation of the downtown district by the business community, especially through the growth of headquarters

Promotion of internal venturing activities within established corporations

Attraction of foreign investors, specially U.S. headquarters of European and Japanese firms entering the U.S. market

Lobbying activities in Washington, the federal capital, and Harrisburg, the state capital

Table 7–2
Employment and Growth Rates in High-Technology Sectors in Philadelphia, 1975–1985

Sector	Employment			Growth Rate	
	1975	1980	1985	1975–80	1980–85
Total Employment	1,780,500	1,922,800	2,046,600	1.55%	1.26%
Manufacturing	458,662	447,654	393,716	−0.48	−2.54
High technology	146,127	146,827	154,983	0.10	0.99
Largest Sectors					
Computer services and data processing	5,914	9,843	19,407	10.73	13.14
Communications equipment	13,917	11,762	18,255	−3.31	8.32
Pharmaceuticals	13,714	15,165	17,998	2.03	3.16
Subtotal	33,545	36,770	55,660	1.85	7.83
Large Sectors					
Office and computing machines	11,872	11,746	13,166	−0.21	2.10
Measuring devices	12,517	14,533	10,405	3.03	−5.89
Electrical components	5,165	8,172	8,978	9.61	1.72
Petroleum refining	8,551	8,623	8,932	0.17	0.64
Space vehicles	3,803	5,605	7,565	8.07	5.60
Aircraft and parts	5,751	6,080	7,454	1.12	3.77
Subtotal	47,659	54,759	56,500	2.82	0.57
Medium Sectors					
Plastics and synthetics	9,757	4,847	5,644	−13.06	2.81
Industrial organic chemicals	2,210	4,687	4,764	16.23	0.30
Electrical transportation equipment	10,825	7,260	3,915	−7.68	−10.62
Special industrial machines	5,931	5,491	3,576	−1.53	−7.50
Electrical industrial equipment	3,466	4,033	3,278	3.08	−3.70

Medical instruments	2,815	4,225	3,200	8.46	−4.93
Miscellaneous chemicals	3,444	3,680	3,149	1.33	−2.79
Engineering and laboratory equipment	1,463	1,044	2,784	−6.53	19.52
Industrial inorganic chemicals	3,502	3,485	2,240	−0.10	−7.72
Subtotal	43,413	38,752	32,550	−2.25	−3.12
Small Sectors					
Engines and turbines	7,940	5,047	1,821	−8.66	−16.92
Soaps and cleaners	1,926	1,977	1,592	0.52	−3.86
Paint	2,823	2,152	1,448	−5.28	−6.95
Radio and TV equipment	2,303	2,022	1,438	−2.57	−6.01
Miscellaneous electrical machinery	2,410	1,642	1,435	−7.39	−2.42
Photography equipment	741	750	886	0.24	3.08
Ordinance and accessories	1,284	871	734	−7.47	−3.06
Agricultural chemicals	1,081	813	524	−5.54	−7.68
Optical instruments	1,002	1,272	395	4.89	−19.15
Subtotal	21,510	16,546	10,273	−5.11	−8.30

Source: Anita Summers, University of Pennsylvania, 1987.

Modification of lending practices of commercial banks to serve young and growing enterprises

Due to the examination of these diverse issues, support for economic development is now better articulated by public and private organizations that coordinate strategies and programs. Among them are: the Greater Philadelphia First Corporation, the Chamber of Commerce, and the Greater Philadelphia Economic Development Coalition.

Building upon the Intellectual Resources of the Region

The metropolitan Philadelphia region has the ability to produce the technical outputs that lead to growth of high technology. While Philadelphia shows a lower than average concentration of workers with science and engineering-related Ph.Ds, at the same time, the area contains an extensive university system. Advanced degrees are awarded by forty-eight institutions of higher education. Estimates place enrollment at about 162,000 full-time students. Medical universities in the metropolitan Philadelphia region provide a base of excellent quality for service and business formation. In biotechnology, one finds two of the largest private life science (DuPont) and biomedical (SmithKline Beckman) laboratories. Medical and biotechnology fields require strengths in bioengineering, pharmaceuticals, chemical engineering, and molecular biology.

Philadelphia's engineering research institutions have strengths in the following areas: materials engineering and processing, chemicals and chemical processing, electronic instruments, physics, and computers and software. Princeton's Supercomputer Consortium was designed to undertake basic research in large capacity computing and fifth-generation computers.

There are many government and non-profit research institutes in Greater Philadelphia. The University City Science Center in Philadelphia and the Forestal Center in Princeton stand out as national leaders. The University Science Center's Research Institutes Division has focused on bioprocessing and pharmaceutical research. Forestal Center's specialties are biotechnology and computers, especially large supercomputers.

Expansion of Existing Firms in the Region

The expansion of established corporations in industries that experienced growth was a critical factor that led to job creation and opened up numerous opportunities for suppliers, parts manufacturers, and support services. In fact, the presence of pharmaceutical firms facing demand growth, such as SmithKline Beckman, and Rohm & Hass, was extremely important in providing economic opportunities in the 1970s and early 1980s.

In the late 1970s, established defense and aerospace, pharmaceutical, and chemicals firms successfully expanded. Chemicals in general, and drugs and pharmaceuticals specifically, were the highest growth areas and the only areas in which Philadelphia's regional growth was greater than that of the United States as a whole. Other relatively strong industries during that period included office and computing equipment; radio and TV equipment; wholesale and retail trade, insurance, finance, and business services; utilities; and communication and computer services.

It is generally agreed amongst business leaders in Philadelphia that the expansion of major established companies in the 1970s and early 1980s accounts for approximately 70 percent of new employment in the manufacturing and service sectors. The attraction of branch plants from corporations located outside the region was not a very successful avenue, except the arrival of Kodak's pharmaceutical division in 1987.

The Availability of Venture Capital

An example of the improvisations that have to be made to build the necessary infrastructure for high technology is the development of venture capital in the Philadelphia area. Both the Chamber of Commerce and the Philadelphia Partnership agreed that the lack of venture capital in the 1970s was inhibiting the creation and expansion of firms. A number of studies demonstrated the low level of venture capital activity. For example, a survey conducted by the University City Science Center indicated that none of the tenants had found venture capital in Philadelphia. Another survey, sponsored by the Wharton Innovation Center, noted that virtually none of the forty-two firms sampled was backed by local venture firms.

In the early 1980s, it was agreed that action was needed. A number of funds were set up by established corporations: the largest venture capital fund was established by SmithKline Beckman Corporation for investment in health-related start-ups and expansions. Many CEOs of large firms decided to institute similar funds. Finally, the absence of local venture-capital expertise was reversed, not only by attracting offices of national venture capital firms, but also by attracting venture capitalists to Philadelphia. As a result, several venture capital funds, worth about $220 million, have been established. The Delaware Valley Venture Group links the thirty venture-capital firms in the area and provides a forum to discuss problems and initiatives.

State Support for High Technology

State programs to support the introduction of advanced manufacturing technologies and the promotion of start-ups have also been ingredients in the rejuvenation process of the metropolitan Philadelphia region. A conscious effort was made to reduce taxes and adopt a non-interventionist posture.

The Ben Franklin Partnership, established to provide public funds for

R&D and product development projects, is credited by many business executives as a model of supportive state action. Initiated by Governor Dick Thornburgh in 1982, the Partnership's major action is four Advanced Technology Centers, each representing a consortium of research universities, private business, labor, and economic development groups. Since 1982, $60 million in state funding was leveraged with consortium matching funding of $170 million, making the Partnership the largest state technology development program in the United States. Close to four hundred projects are being supported in 1986. Each of the four centers provides:

> joint applied-research and development efforts with the private sector, in specified areas such as robotics, biotechnology, and (CAD/CAM);

> education and training, assisting all higher educational institutions to provide training.

Conclusion

The rejuvenation of Greater Philadelphia through high technology is far from complete. Although Philadelphia has many assets, nurturing new firm development remains difficult. The Philadelphia region must still overcome vestiges of conservative business traditions and must provide more resources to the rapidly growing high-technology sector. Role models must be developed within the academic and business communities to spur entrepreneurship.

Part IV
Developing Effective Strategies for Economic Development Through High Technology

Strategies to accelerate the development and growth of high-technology clusters can be effective only if they are in agreement with the underlying dynamics of economic growth. Such strategies should aim to build the infrastructure and secure the commitment of parties that can make things happen. However, such strategies need not only a long-term horizon but a continued focus over the years, despite changing leadership.

Chapter 8 highlights the pitfalls of strategies that peg hopes on "quick fix" solutions such as "seek and find programs," incubators, centers of excellence, technology parks, and picking winners. Chapter 9 sketches the elements and programs that can form the underpinning of public–private partnerships for building the infrastructure and for activating the processes that will enhance the rate of business formation, whether by entrepreneurs or corporate venture groups.

8
Mirages and Pitfalls

Many errors are made in the well-intentioned pursuit of economic development. Recourse to simplistic strategies that do not rest on solid experience lead many communities astray. Government officials, community leaders, and business persons often fall for mirages that promise jobs and high-technology plants, but have little chance of significant job creation.

Good intentions do not necessarily lead to economic development. Moreover, well-intentioned measures and policies, which are efficient in specific contexts and at particular times, tend to be promoted widely. Dressed up as grandiose strategies, they are bound to fail because they are inappropriate in different contextual situations. We will review five of these strategies: "seek and find" programs, incubators and technology centers, university-based industrial strategies, technology parks, and picking the winners.

Initiatives along these lines are not necessarily wrong. In fact, they may constitute valid programs within a coherent strategy. However, when pursued alone, in many circumstances, they will be inefficient and irrelevant to the process of economic growth. Thus, it is important to understand what makes them work and what their limitations are.

Buying Your Way: The "Seek and Find" Approach to Economic Development

The most common misconception about economic development is the idea that growth depends on attracting industries from outside the area. The pursuit of initiatives of this sort is depicted by the well-known image of the industrial commissioner, the mayor, the commerce secretary, or even the governor, who put on their "salesman suit" and take to the road to extoll the virtues of "home" as "the" place to invest and to establish "your" next plant. "Come and see us," tout the full-page advertisements in business publications. Most of these efforts and the funds spent to sustain them could be invested more efficiently in other ways. Indeed, the relatively minor importance of branch plants is often ignored by professionals and business executives involved in economic development.

Branch plants are set up by corporations that operate more than one physical plant or establishment. These corporations account for 70 percent of jobs in the private sector. Conversely, 30 percent of the jobs in the private sector are in single establishment business. Thus, most jobs in the market place are in corporations with more than one establishment. Most multi-unit establishments are branches serving local markets. Typical "branches" may be a Humana hospital, an IBM regional sales office, a McDonald's restaurant, a Procter and Gamble regional distribution center, a Sears store, or a Shell service station. These locally oriented establishments are set up in an area to tap the potential of local markets. In technical terms, they are "induced" by the local economy.

Efforts are rarely needed to attract these "induced" establishments to a region. No promotion is needed. Decision-makers are attracted by the potential of the local market. Sometimes, two areas within a regional market compete. For instance, two suburbs can aim at attracting a shopping center or a regional distribution center. But the decision to tap a given regional market with a new establishment usually depends little on efforts of civic boosters. Depending on the economic structure of a region, between 60 percent and 80 percent of jobs are in the local sector. Furthermore, over 60 percent of jobs in multi-establishment corporations are tied to serving the local market.

But not all establishments are tied to local markets. Some establishments are said to belong to the economic base of a region and are oriented toward wider national or international markets. Branch plants such as an IBM facility manufacturing wafers, a Sanders Associates' instrumentation plant, and a Martin Marietta components plant are typical of these establishments. "Basic" establishments are found mostly in the manufacturing sector. However, more and more service-oriented basic establishments are appearing, such as an airline central reservation center or a bank card central processing establishment. Manufacturing and service basic plants employ approximately 25 percent of the total U.S. labor force in the private sector. These are the targets of "seek and find" strategies. They are not bounded by the need to serve a local market because their products or services are delivered to a much wider market place. Moreover, they belong to corporations that operate more than one plant, sometimes in many states or countries.

"Seek and find" strategies are involved in a tough and highly competitive game. New basic branch plants do not generate a large proportion of new jobs in the economy. Branch plants in manufacturing represented a small proportion of the total increase in manufacturing employment in the seven year period extending from 1969 to 1976. Most of the new manufacturing jobs came from single-establishment manufacturing companies and from expansions of existing plants. A small percentage of the new jobs created in North America result from new manufacturing branch plants. High-technology branch plants represent less than 0.5 percent. Thus, chasing high-technology branch plants is very much like looking for a needle in a hay stack. One questions whether the time spent pursuing a limited number of high-technology branch plants represents a useful investment of effort and resources.

Nevertheless, a significant number of jobs is involved. For instance, if 2 million jobs are created in a typical year in the United States, new high-tech branch plants can represent up to 10,000 new jobs. This is not to be neglected. These jobs will be housed in 50 to 75 new plants of 150 to 250 employees. "Seek and find" programs chase them and deem them sufficiently attractive.

But here is the bad news. For most corporations, the best place to locate a new branch plant is in a neighborhood with existing manufacturing plants. To the question, "Where should we locate this new plant?" most executives will finally answer, "Nearby." We estimate that at least half of new branch plants are located "nearby." A number of factors explain this preference. First, corporations possess information about issues such as the availability of workers, the presence of good real-estate developers, and the preferences of employees for areas in which they currently operate. Second, corporations benefit from their present bases of operations in the start-up phase of any new plant. Proximity greatly facilitates the execution of expansion plans—from hiring and training of workers to supervising the lay-out of machinery and equipment. Third, the logistics of exchanges between the network of plants are easier if the new plant is in the same general area. Also, "action" attracts the attention of corporations. Most corporations will prefer areas where competitors are established. In such agglomerations, they know that they will find skilled workers and experienced subcontractors.

As a consequence, plants of multi-establishment corporations tend to be concentrated in a single broad area. Digital Equipment Corporation's plants are around Boston; Rohlm's plants are spread in the Santa Clara county; General Electric has several plants in southeastern Pennsylvania, and Westinghouse is in southwestern Pennsylvania.

"Nearby" is an important criteria for plants that have to maintain close technical and commercial relationships with sister plants. On the other hand, "sterile" plants, which are self-enclosed and entertain few critical exchanges with the business environment, can be shipped off much more easily to sites elsewhere in the country. Our estimate is that there are probably twenty-five to thirty-five foot-loose high-technology plants looking for a "home" in a typical year in North America. This is not a big number. Yet, these plants are up for grabs and several "lucky" communities will host them.

A corporation in the position of "siting" a foot-loose plant will consider many factors if it has rejected "nearby" as a solution. Let us look at how such choices are made.

A corporation might locate a manufacturing plant in a specific area for political and marketing reasons. Most corporations prefer areas that develop rapidly and have established competitors. The mere presence of competitors affects the cost structure. Thus, development breeds its own momentum. An East Coast-based computer manufacturer may want to have a presence in Santa Clara County on the West Coast and vice-versa; many Santa Clara-based manufacturers have established some operations in New England. The location of Kodak's new pharmaceutical division in Philadelphia is an example of locating where the "action" is, where an agglomeration of pharmaceutical firms has grown.

Moving with the marketplace is another strategic reason. Many manufacturers of consumer products will attempt to follow the general shift in population and the national market when expanding production capacity. Minimizing costs is another basic motive that shapes location decisions. Low-cost, nonunionized labor has often been said to be a key advantage of the southern states. Highly skilled productive labor, availability of experienced suppliers, proximity of markets, and cheap energy are used to promote various areas. Grants, from subsidized land to tax-exempt bonds and free public amenities, are also used with increasing frequency.

Once the region has been selected, many subsidiary factors will be considered: the friendliness of the people, the persistence of the promoter, and the general appearance of the site. These factors can play a determining role when picking a location from among competitive sites a few miles apart.

"Seek and find" strategies are thus high-risk development strategies, and most communities are losers. Development strategies that rely on attracting branch plants are seldom successful, although on the surface many appear to be. In fact, when plants, offices, and warehouses with a local orientation are excluded, not many cities and counties are successful with "seek and find" strategies.

"Seek and find" strategies are successful in limited circumstances. The following conditions contribute to the success of such a strategy in an area.

1. The area is located in a growth region. In particular, communities with good "seek and find" potential are within or near a major metropolitan area with significant growth potential or are located in a region that is expected to maintain a superior rate of growth during the next ten to twenty years.

2. The area offers relatively lower-cost conditions for manufacturing operations. When a manufacturer feels constrained by its present sites, expansion of facilities in areas where costs can be minimized will be sought.

Central geographic locations, absence of unions, low taxes, and low energy costs will be positive factors.

3. For high-technology industries, the presence of a cluster of high-technology firms ensures an adequate local supply of workers, suppliers, and subcontractors. High-technology firms employ two types of workers: highly skilled workers, such as engineers and scientists, and assembly-line workers. Moving into an area where a cluster is already established ensures that this particular mix will be found.

The "landing" of distribution centers, regional offices, and plants directed at the local market often passes as examples of "seek and find" success. In reality, these establishments were attracted to the area by demand conditions, that is, local-market opportunities. The decision to settle in a particular region is usually independent of the efforts of local promoters. What "seek and find" efforts can sometime do is accelerate corporate decisions by one or two fiscal years, or influence the details of siting.

Only a few regions have what it takes to succeed in the "seek and find." The southern part of the United States, the West Coast, and selected pockets in the Northeast and Midwest have the right mix of long-term attractiveness in terms of growth and cost structures. They have the fundamentals required to play the highly competitive game of attracting "foot-loose" plants.

However, what they get is not as attractive as it looks on the surface. A branch plant is typically a well-designed operation geared toward maximum efficiency. It does not grow easily. Building another plant elsewhere is often more efficient than adding capacity. Moreover, branch plants often house the routine or low-skill end of high-technology activities. An R&D center is not as foot-loose as an assembly line. Success in attracting branch plants means gaining an assembly line without much brainpower attached to it.

Remember that quite often these plants are sterile and contribute little to the dynamics of future growth. They have few activities that incubate future entrepreneurs. They do not entertain autonomous relations with suppliers. They are seldom involved in product design. Because marketing and sales are managed elsewhere, branch plants do not interact with the marketplace. Their design for efficiency lowers the probability of sprawling growth. Only plants engaged in product development can eventually trigger a process of local growth.

Millions are being spent annually by cities, counties, and states to lure new establishments. Some big successes (there are a few that spring up once in a while) are achieved. The lucky communities will surely say that their advertising campaign helped them by laying the ground work. In fact, a strong advertising compaign increases the probability that a city or a county will be on the *short list* of candidates whenever a corporation comes in the area. Bloomington, Minnesota gets on the short list nearly as often as Minneapolis or St. Paul. Once an area is in the short list, it has a fighting chance. Millions of dollars are thus spent to lure plants fifty miles away. This inefficient zero-sum game is nevertheless the flashiest game in town.

Incubators: First or Second Generation

The latest fad in economic development is providing incubator space to assist start-up businesses in their first years of operations. The incubator provides start-ups with low-cost space and services, contacts, advice, and guidance. Enterprise Centers are a variant of the same concept, coming into play at the pre-start-up stage where would-be entrepreneurs can tap the technological resources of a cooperative university to develop product ideas, build prototypes, and prepare the business plans to obtain funds and start a business.

The concept is intellectually appealing, and communities, universities, and businesses may consider it a public service. The promise of success has made incubators and enterprise centers the most popular local development tools presently promoted across North America. In a sense, the fashion of incubators and enterprise centers reminds us of the brisk popularity enjoyed by industrial parks in the early 1960s and by industrial commissioners a few years later. These two new ideas were supposed to contribute significantly to the spread of industrial development. Incubators have now come of age. Industrial and office park real-estate developers now include incubator space and services in their new multi-tenant buildings. A few corporations have also been established to sell incubators to communities across North America, sometimes for development purposes, often times, to sweeten the pill of plant closures.

Are incubators cornucopias from which will flow continuous streams of healthy new enterprises? Or are they, as industrial parks and commissioners were, just tools, albeit useful ones, for industrial development? We tend to think the latter. An incubator can play a useful role in industrial development. But its usefulness is nevertheless significantly limited because of the nature of entrepreneurship and the particularities of building a new business, which cannot always be reconciled with frameworks of incubators and enterprise centers.

To capture an opportunity, an entrepreneur gathers, over time, a set of physical, technological, and financial resources and combines them to insert a new activity into the economy. To be successful, the new activity as a result of its unique combination of cost and product attributes must be competitive with alternatives presently offered in the marketplace. Otherwise, the activity will not be profitable, and resources will eventually be drained out, forcing the business to close down.

Entrepreneurs come in various types. Classifications all have limitations, but they sometimes help in understanding a phenomena. For the purposes at hand, we will classify entrepreneurs in two categories: those who come up with a better "mouse trap" and those who simply provide a mouse trap when it is needed. The McDonald franchise belongs to the second category. A good operator can manage successfully thirty-five to forty employees. The first type of entrepreneur shows more imagination: he is the designer of a better mouse trap and dreams of proving to the world that he too can "make it." Great entrepreneurs belong to this group. Ray Kroc, who invented McDonald's, is the epitome of the better mouse trap builder: he perfected the cornerstore restaurant.

High-technology entrepreneurs are innovators who offer, in a given market, a superior product or service. However, to be a successful entrepreneur, one needs more than a better idea. The idea has to be translated into a product or service, at a competitive price. Furthermore, it has to be marketed to its targeted customers. To do that, the entrepreneur has to build and lead an organization.

Entrepreneurs are much more than "idea persons" who have the determination and the resources to take up the challenge of starting a business. Successful entrepreneurs have to be managers and builders of organizations. Moreover, as the organization grows, the management problems facing the entrepreneur will change. Thus, entrepreneurs have to evolve and rely on new skills as their firms grow.

The ideal entrepreneur rarely exists, but entrepreneurial firms manage to live with non-perfect entrepreneurs. They compensate their deficiencies with teams and strengths in other areas. Many organizations have learned to cope with their founders' poor managerial skills and with deficient managerial resources at the top. The overall mix of abilities and skills turn out to be sufficient for success.

The motive behind the establishment of an incubator is to provide some compensating assets to entrepreneurs at the most critical phase, that is, at the start-up period. The logic is simple. If the difficulties of these first years could be eased, less fatalities would occur. Furthermore, more would-be entrepreneurs would venture as they would feel more secure inside an incubator.

Unfortunately, in the desire to avoid fatalities, many errors are committed. Why have incubators not set ablaze industrial development? There must be weaknesses to the concept. Indeed, experience indicates that four fundamental weaknesses are becoming evident in the incubators presently in operation.

First, over time, incubators tend to emphasize the office management functions to the detriment of the entrepreneurial support functions. Most incubators start with strong desires to offer entrepreneurial support. However, the mission usually shifts over with the emphasis on the provision of common services and space management. Two fundamental reasons bring about this change in priorities. First, the day-to-day pressures are exerted by tenants who expect high-quality common services. At any point in time, what the majority of tenants wants is water in the fountain, a clean conference room, the receptionist arriving on time, and so on. The need to meet these expectations puts pressure to hire a general manager, somebody who can "run the shop" in a proper fashion. The majority of the tenants who provide the bread and butter income of the incubators insist on it. The ability to provide entrepreneurial support then takes the back seat when the time comes to attend office management responsibilities.

The provision of entrepreneurial support services, from preparing a business place to scrounging for funds, loans, grants, and equity, requires substantial time and effort from the promoters who initially supported the incubators. Failures are bound to occur. Desperate efforts are made to save a failing business. These intense periods are hard on the day-to-day operations of the incubator. Only a few cases can be handled in one year. Moreover, after a while, most "angels" quit. Volunteer businessmen tend to focus on other projects. General managers also quit to take less stressful jobs. Office managers then take over and the emphasis on entrepreneurial support diminishes.

Second, the need of equity and capital occurs not only at the start-up period. Firms go usually through a series of financing rounds over the first few years of operation. Success must have been achieved to get new funds. Business plans are revised under the watchful eyes of investors. Entrepreneurs who need help in making a business plan will not impress investors. Furthermore, investors usually monitor strategic moves and decisions to ensure that past investments are safeguarded. Incubator managers and "angels" cannot provide on a sustained basis the ongoing involvement in strategic decisions that a venture capitalist will find normal. For instance, incubator managers and volunteer businessmen will not fire a vice president or reverse entrepreneurs' decisions easily. The venture capitalist will.

Third, incubators tend to attract and retain low-potential "problem" firms. The astute observer who visits a mature incubator is overwhelmed by the low-growth potential of most businesses found there. Although the patterns vary with each type of incubator, this observation applies to offices, R&D, and manufacturing incubators alike. For instance, not-for-profit research organizations and advocacy organizations thrive in "office" incubators. So do the one person operations whose offices are closed most of the time. In "manufacturing" incubators, local service or subcontract firms dominate. These firms seldom die, but they will never go anywhere either.

The feeling that one is not "where the action is" grabs any astute observer walking through an incubator. Incubators do not attend to the future leaders of industrial America. They are too busy looking after the free-riders and the problem firms.

Fourth, incubators lack one of the most important benefits sought by real entrepreneurs: social recognition. An incubator is egalitarian: long corridors with doors every thirty feet with third-rate signs on most of them, announcing little two-bit operations. This is not a neighborhood for high-powered entrepreneurs. The real entrepreneur secretly dreams of having his corporate logo perched high "up there," showing the world with bravado how well he made it in the tough world of high technology. An incubator does not recognize this aspect of an entrepreneur's inner world. There are major motivational drawbacks to the common reception area, the haphazard physical mix of tenants along drab corridors, and the lack of attention to public recognition. Industrial real-estate developers do not make that mistake. They know what to offer: individual entry with a few parking spaces for the president and "visitor," a glass front door, options for hanging the corporate logo, or the corner office with a bay window for the president. These are little details that really count. After all, why do you think entrepreneurs log in those fifteen-hour days?

The present infatuation with incubators will cool off as results unfold or fail to occur over time. Moreover, real-estate developers will gradually co-opt the concept and offer "incubator" services in their multi-tenants buildings. Many not-for-profit incubators, with unsound financial structure, will encounter financial difficulties. In fact, many incubators are already encountering leasing problems, even those in operation for years.

Leasing space and offering common office services to small businesses is a rather mundane business activity that can best be carried by real-estate managers. Offering technical assistance and advice to small businesses can be offered by many professionals or by industrial development agencies. "Incubator" organizations provide these services unwillingly or voluntarily at times. What matters most is the quality of the services rendered. That such services are needed and important to new businesses is undeniable. Whether incubator organizations will have the financial back-bone and the commitment to fulfill this mission over many years is uncertain. Some incubators will succeed in this important task.

High-Technology Parks

High-technology parks were promoted in the 1960s and 1970s as efficient tools for the development of high-technology industries. Parks were seen as a place to transfer R&D results from universities and research centers by high-technology firms established within them.

Results have been disappointing. The North American experience with research and technology parks indicates that a majority of these have been failures. Few of them have succeeded in generating a self-sustaining process of growth leading to continued new business creation. Among the approximate 150 high-technology parks that exist, few are considered successes or partial successes.

The MIT Technology Square was conceived in the early 1960s as an incubator of high-technology start-ups near the MIT campus. The promoters of the project at MIT soon realized that the original building stood empty as entrepreneurs preferred cheaper Crane Trust buildings, or conventional industrial parks along Route 128. MIT's president then contacted the president of IBM, who located an R&D project in the building. Another building was later built for NASA.

The Technology Square project is now occupied by three major tenants with long-term leases: Polaroid Corporation, MIT's Information Systems Institute, and Draper Laboratories. Technology Square is now owned by Prudential Insurance and managed by a real-estate developer. Technology Square never became a hot bed for new high-technology companies founded by entrepreneurs associated with MIT.

Learning from its incubator and innovation center experiences, MIT is now turning to the private sector for the redevelopment of the Simplex area in Cambridge. The University Park is presently being developed over an area of 725,000 square feet as an office R&D park. MIT has selected a national real-estate developer to do the planning, building, and marketing of the park on land leased by MIT. The interactions between the developer and MIT are designed in such a way as to minimize the involvement of MIT and its research institutes and departments. An MIT vice president for real estate approves any tenant leasing over 25,000 square feet. The first tenants were not high-technology firms but architectural and engineering firms.

Given the original objectives, more than 50 percent of technology parks can be considered outright failures. They have not succeeded in attracting a significant number of tenants. The parks that are considered successful have attracted mostly large organizations, which have set up laboratories and special projects, and sometimes, research-oriented divisions. Government offices and service firms have also located in these parks. Jobs and high-technology activities have been established near universities. On the other hand, research and technology parks have contributed little to the process of net new job creation. Most organizations locating in these parks would have located nearby anyway. These organizations were not born due to the technology parks. Few start-ups and spin-offs can be traced back and attributed directly to the institutional support found in research and technology parks.

Three major lessons can be learned from the experience of high-technology parks. First, developing a research and technology park is a long-term process requiring a long-term commitment. Planning horizons of twenty to thirty years are not uncommon. Second, university-related research parks are particularly difficult to develop because of the conflicting expectations of the diverse interests that promote them. Third, very few, if any, university-related research or technology parks have succeeded in creating a self-sustaining process of growth. University affiliation is good for image building. However, relations between tenants, university departments, and institutes are seldom highly productive.

Ivory Towers in the Industrial Realm

Enterprise development centers (EDCs) are creations of ambitious deans of engineering schools. They are cousins of incubators. An EDC targets product ideas, usually in the area of high technology, and aims at bringing them into real-life products around which new businesses will be built. An EDC is usually established as an extension of an engineering or biology school. Professors and graduate students work in EDCs, sometimes on their own, sometimes under contract with an outside business. The development is usually funded by government programs. Funding also covers the preparation of business plans and the inevitable marketing studies, which are usually done at the friendly local business schools.

EDCs aim to build bridges between universities and the business world, allowing the latter to tap the research done at the universities. EDCs rest on the premise that faculty members have entrepreneurial talent and are disciplined engineers who can efficiently translate technical ideas into marketable products. Various types of EDCs can be found from the grandiose high-technology strategies hatched by blue ribbon committees with strong ties to universities to more realistic projects.

Cautious analysts of the university-industry-government cooperation in research and technology transfer have more realistic hopes for technology centers. The expected short-term benefit is better communication between universities and businesses. What often occurs is that, instead of the universities hatching new businesses, established businesses contribute to raising the standards of education and research at engineering schools. In the medium term, universities will get revenues from patents and licenses as faculty members get involved in product development efforts. In the long term, new firms may emerge as some entrepreneurs will exploit product development concepts or patented technologies.

There is merit in developing ties between universities and the high-technology community to increase exchanges. But there are several ways by which transfers can be done. Graduate students migrating to local firms, while keeping ties with former colleagues and professors, are a most common way of establishing linkages. Consulting contracts link professors and researchers to high-technology firms. Research can also be contracted out. However, not many firms will use outside suppliers or professors, except under unusual circumstances, for critical R&D. Product development is a highly competitive tool for a technology firm. Most firms are not about to subcontract strategic tasks to researchers who do not have solid performance records.

Universities create problems in the development of regional high-technology strategies. First, universities are usually well represented in the task forces that design strategies. Furthermore, professors are articulate and usually speak with authority on these subjects. They seem to own high technology: they usually have strong interests to promote. What universities are in fact pursuing with regional high-technology strategies is more state funding to replace dwindling federal funds. In particular, funding for EDCs and the like are frequently demanded.

The second problem has to do with the general inefficiency of universities as incubators of entrepreneurs. It is not that university professors do not have their fair share of entrepreneurship. Indeed, one can think of many departments that attract entrepreneurially oriented graduate students. The main drawback of universities is their distance from the market place. Professors and graduate students are not motivated by the imperative need to earn a living and to work on problems that have marketable applications. In spite of the new rhetorical discourse, university cultures view business as too close to the marketplace. In fact, one of the most revealing symptoms of this distance is the type of projects that are pursued in EDCs. The majority of projects have no real commercial relevance, at least to hard-nosed entrepreneurs. The fact that very few of these projects find commercial sponsors ready to commit funds is a good indicator of their commercial relevance.

The best contribution that a technologically oriented university can make to the local development of high technology is to be a center of educational and research excellence in leading fields. As a second major contribution, it can impart entrepreneurial attitudes to graduate students by promoting linkages through summer and part-time jobs and research contracts. In fact, this was the major contribution of Stanford University to Silicon Valley. Such a view of the university respects the basic division of roles in our industrial society rather than blurring roles.

Picking the Winners

If one is to believe the folklore, there exists within the Japanese Ministry of International Trade (MITI) an army of enlightened bureaucrats deciphering the technologies that turn out to be winners. In fact, Japan's success in various high-technology areas rests on many reasons, one of which may not be the guiding light of bureaucrats. Japan's fierce competition in its domestic markets has fostered uniquely innovative organizations, which are quite good at incremental progress. The ability of Japanese firms to borrow and adapt foreign technologies and do away with the NIH (Not Invented Here) syndrome is well-known. Japanese industrial corporations have used public funds efficiently to spread risks in the development of technologies.

"Picking winners" is the ultimate illusion of industrial strategists. The positive aspect of a market economy is that failures usually get weeded out before becoming too visible. In Canada, the federal government has poured several billion dollars into development of what the bureaucrats assured us was the best, most secure, and efficient nulcear reactor technology in the world. Building on national pride, they managed to sell the technology to various provincial governments. Overseas, three reactors were sold with heavy subsidies. Many European governments have put hopes on similar high-technology projects.

The problem with "picking winners" strategies does not only lie in their batting averages, which tend to be rather poor. Winners turn out usually to be privately owned corporations. Bureaucrats displace then their ardor for whole industrial sectors. Winners become faceless, but politically acceptable, technologies. Since no direct accounting is kept, the cost–benefit of these technological choices is never established *ex post facto*.

Venture capitalists are in the business of picking the winners of tomorrow and the organizations with leadership and technology. On the whole, the venture capital industry does its job adequately, even if, at times, mistakes are made. Cases of overinvestments do occur, the Winchester Disk Drive industry is an example. What a venture capitalist cannot do is grow artificial "winners," or even build winners. They pick winners and often err in trying to do it.

Conclusion

A common characteristic of all simplistic strategies is the desire for quick results. With elections every four years, the pattern is established to sustain high-profile public initiatives. Unfortunately, four years will never be enough time. A longer time horizon is needed to develop a self-sustaining high-technology cluster.

The same applies to the development of a base of new firms. Incubators are also quick-fix solutions. Entrepreneurs do not need $2.00 per square foot space. After all, they are good calculators, and such offers are not deciding factors. Instead, one has to instill the entrepreneurial spirit in incubating organizations, where the entrepreneurs of tomorrow presently make their living. Success stories will get their attention. The possibility of landing contracts will make them consider taking the big leap. The availability of a second partner, who has seen it before in many other ventures, will appeal to them. These are the fundamental factors that nourish the growth of high-technology clusters.

9

A Development Strategy

development strategy is, above all, a shared vision of what the future can be, as well as a dedication by the private and public leaders to achieve this vision. Its aim is to insure coherence among policies and continuity of effort over time to minimize conflictual, counterintuitive, and inefficient moves.

Whatever its internal coherence and elegance or its short-term appeal, no strategy can change the reality of the development process. The emergence of a high-technology cluster results from a gradual build-up of activities by corporate ventures and start-ups spread over several decades. Nonetheless, a long-term strategy can be designed and implemented in a region, either to accelerate the process or to build the basic institutional conditions.

Realistic Development Objectives

A strategy aims at reaching some objectives. Thus, setting the objectives must precede the strategy. Realistic objectives are not necessarily humble. On the contrary, realistic objectives can embody ideals such as the creation of a milieu in which challenging jobs are offered to coming generations, the promotion of individual responsibility for creating one's job, and the development of an environment that allows the exercise of individual creativity, thus bringing the human being to its full potential. What makes objectives realistic is their conformity to the reality of the process of economic development.

Thus, a realistic objective represents a vision of a better future for the whole community. Not all objectives meet this criteria. In fact, the major criticism levelled at many community and government intervention programs to stimulate high technology is that they are basically costly zero-sum games. Nationally, the competition for branch plants is obviously a zero-sum game that has a redistribution effect between regions. At the regional level, the competition for new businesses between suburbs and the city area through incentives to business is also a zero-sum game.

The objectives of economic development through high technology should go beyond the zero-sum game to achieve not only growth but real development. Two avenues of development can be pursued. The first type is for a community with little or no high-technology activities; the second is for the vast majority of large cities which, as our data showed in chapter 2, already possess some high-technology base.

A community with few high-technology activities and without the basic infrastructure could focus on the modest objective of building up a base of technology users. Eventually, a critical mass of such users would be achieved, and the agglomeration could start generating local spin-offs.

Bootstrapping operations are likely to be costly, extend over a long period of time, and yield few agglomeration effects. Moreover, the attracted branch plants are likely to consist of the low end of high technology, with few design and research activities being conducted there. It is worth noting that after more than thirty years of operations, the Research Triangle Park, which is composed mostly of research and manufacturing branch plants, cannot be said to have achieved a self-sustaining status.

The second avenue, which is recommended to most agglomerations of significant size, aims at building a diverse and self-sustaining cluster in which new local firms in emerging high-technology sectors replace decaying firms or the branching out of establishments. One of the difficulties associated with an economic strategy aimed at growth industries through high technology is the inability to forecast with any assurance which industries will grow in the future. In view of the difficulty of forecasting the industrial and employment potentials of technologies, a strategy that aims at creating a self-sustaining process should focus on the conditions leading to the formation, survival, and growth of new ventures. Multiplying the number of entrepreneurial and corporate ventures will eventually lead to actualized results in spite of failures. Entrepreneurship is widely distributed and can be released by paying attention to the processes that lead to new business formation in the field of high technology.

The objectives of a high-technology development strategy should be to stimulate the rate of business creation by focusing on the processes that support the emergence of new high-technology businesses. Thus, the key to any sound strategy is to trigger or maintain a clustering process with home-grown firms. To achieve this goal, attention will have to be paid to building the technical and business infrastructure as well as to stimulating the process described in chapter 4. A sound development strategy will display the following characteristics:

1. Its planning horizon is long (ten to twenty years), to ensure both continuity in policies and coherence amongst the various moves.

2. Its emphasis is on creating the institutional conditions favorable to the emergence of a high-technology cluster. It does not emphasize direct intervention by governments, but it seeks to marshall in a coherent fashion the support of federal, state, and municipal authorities in the building of the basic institutional conditions.

3. It is directed at activating regional linkages between start-ups and growing new firms on the one hand, and mature firms, financial institutions, universities, and research centers, on the other hand.

4. It relies mainly on home-grown firms, with the emphasis on assisting the emergence and growth of local high-technology firms. When the self-sustaining process is underway, the attraction of new corporate divisions or autonomous branch plants can start to be emphasized.

5. It aims at developing a business climate hospitable to entrepreneurial initiatives in the high-technology area. The thrust of the strategy will be towards stimulating private entrepreneurial actions.

A Public–Private Partnership

Development strategies can be developed by private sector groups and by government officials. Our experience indicates that effective public–private partnerships can, better than other forms, put together the elements of a sound and long-term strategy.

Strategies for the development of high-technology in a region can be designed and implemented from a variety of perspectives, such as:

National policies directed at building the basic research expertise in universities, stimulating the flow of entrepreneurial capital into high risk activities, or influencing the location of defense and aerospace establishments through procurement decisions. National policies cannot *a priori* favor a particular region. Political bargaining over and above the promotion of its intrinsic qualities is obviously necessary for a region to get its share of research centers, procurement contracts and research awards.

State (or provincial) policies to facilitate the flow of equity investments into high-risk ventures, to adequately fund graduate studies and applied research in universities, and to train the staff which high-technology firms need.

Community programs and policies to offer competitive incentives to firms locating in high-technology parks, to build the basic physical infrastructure, and to set up incubator facilities with the hope of stimulating new businesses.

Corporate decisions to encourage internal venture projects and to boost the technological capabilities of the firm through R&D activities, acquisitions, and alliances. Established firms can decide to undertake national or local procurement programs.

Government Interests

The interest of government in the development of high technology—whether at the federal, state or regional level—is easy to understand and defend. The intervention of the central government is articulated on two broad premises. First, support for R&D and technology transfer is said to be appropriate in circumstances where the size of private investments do not generate or disseminate enough technology to serve the public good in the areas of defense, environment, or public health. In fact, the potential social benefits suggest larger-scale efforts. Second, only the central government has the required resources to harness the scientific and industrial capabilities to pursue basic research for the development of technological opportunities that promise to solve national problems in areas like space, advanced manufacturing techniques, commercial aviation, energy, or information networks.

The major arguments for state or local public initiatives rest on positive external effects and the removal of barriers that prevent the efficient working of labor, capital, or information markets. Public initiatives, in support of R&D, education, or availability of venture capital will lead to positive external effects in the long-run that cannot be financed or justified by private actions above. The second argument for local public initiatives is the removal of barriers to entrepreneurial actions, barriers that slow the rate of business creation.

Private Sector Interests

From the point of view of existing business corporations, the arguments for involvement in a development process rest on both self interest and enlightened social responsibility. Taking a narrow utilitarian stance, some may argue that the operations of markets and the private pursuit of opportunities by entrepreneurs do not justify involvement in activities oriented towards the development of high technology. For a corporation, there are also some negative effects. These are obvious in the case of employees who leave with technical and market opportunities to set up their own firms, when these opportunities could be bases for internal corporate ventures. However, when spin-offs and start-ups are based on opportunities that fall outside the strategic scope of the corporation, the negative effects are smaller, even though departures weaken the corporate talent pool. Moreover, frequent departures leading to spin-offs may eventually bias corporate R&D towards short-term activities at the expense of fundamental and applied work on generic technologies.

However, established corporations do benefit from fostering the growth of high technology in the vicinity of their own establishments. For corporations that depend on regional markets, the gains from increased local demand and investment opportunities are evident. Growth means greater demand for financial, consulting, or professional services. Large accounting or law firms support new high technology firms in the hope of building relationships with future large clients.

For corporations which export most of their production, the growth of a regional high-technology sector also offers general advantages:

1. The number of candidates for acquisitions in the region increases;
2. Managers are challenged by the effervescence around them;
3. Exposure to new technologies in the process of diffusion is such that competitiveness can be enhanced;
4. The quality and the size of the manpower pool in the region is enhanced.

This last point cannot be overestimated. No corporation would decide to locate a new plant out in "nowhereland", if the alternative is to locate it in the midst of a growing pool of talent. By contributing to the enrichment of the local high technology fabric, an established firm is a net gainer.

Beyond these business reasons, many business persons are motivated by the ideals of the community and economic development, to create a better place to raise their family. The community remains a powerful value in modern industrial society, in spite of the attraction of cosmopolitan life, corporate loyalty, and professional identification.

Joining Forces in a Public–Private Partnership

A coherent development plan needs to mesh explicitly the various partial strategies and the well-intentioned but fragmented responses of the relevant local parties. Our contention is that the best place to develop such a strategy is through a visible public–private partnership that can harness the analytical and implementation capabilities of the different leaderships involved.

Public–private partnerships are the best method of obtaining public benefits and external effects while tapping both the experimental, incremental, and unplanned initiatives of private actors and the rational planning approaches demanded by public funding. Public–private partnerships are not based on client–supplier or principal–agent relationships. They are rather based on joint and collaborative decision-making, formally embodied in an agreement.

The leadership in such a partnership must rest with the private sector, through the participation of key business executives and entrepreneurs. They provide the credibility and the contacts within the informal structure of the local business community. Governments, on the other hand, provide support by contributing financial resources, by granting the partnership the legal power to undertake particular projects and by insuring that relevant public decisions contribute to build the infrastructure, especially in education and taxation.

Such partnerships may often begin as task forces. However, they eventually need to be structured to survive the vagaries of time and conflict. The partnership should be designed in such a way that it can withstand declining personal interests, political storms, and apparent successes. Furthermore, as former leaders fade away, the partnership has to enlist the participation of new leaders. Government can use its authority to create and fund a non-profit corporate vehicle. The private sector must contribute some funding. It must above all ensure that the voluntary participation of key figures is forthcoming.

The requirements for success for such public–private partnerships are numerous and sometimes contradictory. Private actors or government officials cannot pursue ideological goals. They also have to sacrifice their immediate interests to the long-term interests of the community. Here are some of the difficulties and contradictions encountered by these partnerships.

The partnership has to assemble the decision makers who can effectively leverage their intentions into effective actions, while avoiding becoming an elite group that cannot send clear messages to the communities involved. The idea of development through high technologies has to be sold.

The backing of the political leadership of the state or the region is mandatory, but the partnership has to keep out of politics. Should short-term political considerations dominate, the partnership would be seen as a fad.

The partnership has to analyze process and infrastructure issues that are of strategic importance to the emergence of high-technology firms, while at the same time avoiding pet solutions that have little regard to the problem at hand.

The partnership has to be able to understand the positions of labor, management, and public officials, while at the same time avoid being trapped into ideological discussions or brokerage positions. Selections of visible opinions leaders is thus critical.

The partnership needs to be regional in its composition, while at the same time focused on the competitive position of both the region infrastructure and the differential advantages of its high-technology industries nationally and internationally.

The partnership has to be able to make cold-blooded analyses of the strengths and weaknesses of the region, while at the same time avoid being dazzled by past success or stymied by perceived weaknesses.

The partnership has to build a comprehensive strategy while at the same time distilling a limited number of action priorities that can serve for the initial and long term.

Designing and Implementing the Strategy

The strategic management literature, as well as the model of the emergence of high-technology activities described in part II, offers appropriate conceptual bases on which to articulate the development of the strategy and its implementation programs.

A development strategy is unique, as it is based on the particular industrial or research strengths of a region. Furthermore, it is targeted at competitive advantages to enhance and at gaps to be corrected. To develop and implement a sound economic development strategy, two major operations must be performed:

1. a diagnosis, to take stock of resources and limitations
2. the weaving of particular interventions into a coherent program, both through the years, to accelerate the process of business creation

A Diagnosis of the Starting Point

A good diagnosis of a region requires six to nine months of data gathering, analysis, and testing of major assumptions. The diagnosis can be performed by a staff group or a consultant. However, it cannot be said to be complete until each member of the partnership thoroughly accepts the facts and the conclusions. One of the key difficulties in developing a strategy is the tendency to be dazzled by achievements in fashionable fields of the day (such as robotics, supercomputers, or genetic engineering). What is required instead, is to focus on assessing the relative position of the region and the competitive advantages of the industries and firms that operate there.

The data to undertake the diagnosis will not necessarily be readily available. Very often, it will require novel restructuring of existing information. Pertinent data will emerge from interviews with key leaders in the areas and subjective interpretation of observations. Gathering novel information and getting the facts will also help build a consensus, particularly in the strengths, weaknesses, and potentials of the region.

The diagnosis to be made of a region should look at the key variables identified in part II of this book. The purpose here should not be to write a superficial document for public consumption on incubators, success stories, and sponsorship. On the contrary, the strategy should take a comparative look at all the elements that deal with the processes of new business formation and the conditions for growth. In practical terms, the diagnosis will look at two broad categories of information: the structure and dynamics of the existing industrial base and in particular its high-technology components, and the stock of resources to assess strengths, weaknesses, and differential advantages.

The Industrial Base. One of the objectives of the analysis of the industrial base of the region is to identify the "starting points" of the clustering process. Starting conditions will vary from one region to another. Two broad categories of starting points may be distinguished. In some regions, the industrial agglomeration is composed of numerous high-technology firms and mature technology-based firms. In such a region, the clustering process can be deemed to have already been triggered. In many regions, young high-technology firms will be more limited in number, and by reason of necessity, mature technology-based firms will often form the core of the strategy. These firms could have been former starts in the 1950s or 1960s. In many aspects, their products and processes still incorporate state-of-the-art technology.

The second starting point could be an agglomeration of public laboratories and branch plants. These establishments are not efficient incubators, but low-efficiency incubators are better than nothing. Branch plants and laboratories with world or product development mandates could help compensate the lack of industrial agglomeration laboratories.

The analysis of the existing industrial base will also need to answer the following questions:

1. What are the major high-technology industries in the region?
2. What are the prospects and the probable evolution of the high-technology sectors in which regional firms are active?
3. What has been the rate of business formation and survival in the last quarter of century in each of the major high-technology sectors?
4. What are the competitive positions of major regional firms in each one of these high-technology sectors? What skills and unique advantages do these firms possess? What are the firms in the local market by categories such as financial services, mature industrial sectors, and growing service?
5. What are the abilities of each high-technology, manufacturing, or service

firm, or type of firms, in playing the competitive game nationally or locally? What firms deserve attention, help, or benign neglect? What firms are beyond hope?

6. What is the importance of the indigenous base of small and local high-technology firms, compared to branch plants, mature companies, and established high-technology firms?

Taking Stock of Resources. The design strategy will rest also on a realistic assessment of the potential of a region, especially the presence of incubators and the level of local sponsorship, which reflects on the local availability of initial contracts. The census of the technology-based firms in the region will indicate what level of effervescence is plausible. Thus, beyond a thorough understanding of the industrial base of the region, a judgment has to be passed on other resources that could support high-technology business formation. Here are some issues worth investigating:

1. What is the regional diversity of emerging high-technology sectors in which employment is low but where the potential for new business formation is high?

2. What are the high-technology sectors in which local institutions are active in terms of basic research, applied development venture-capital financing, business creation, business expansions, and employment?

3. What are the comparative strengths and weaknesses of universities in the region in fields that are pertinent to high-technology development: engineering, biology, computer science, agriculture, human and veterinary medicine? How do institutions in the region compare nationally in terms of basic and applied research activities?

4. What firms and institutions have been leading incubators in the last fifteen years? Why have they been good incubators, and will they continue to be? In what proportion are research and manufacturing activities of these incubators government-directed by defense spending and purchasing rather than market forces?

5. What programs have been designed by established firms to stimulate external ventures? Are these programs known to others? What efforts are made by established firms to contract-out locally for high-technology products and services?

6. How active is the formal venture-capital industry in the region? What deals and emerging sectors do they focus upon? Have they had major local success lately? What is the importance of informal venture-capital activity in the region? What networks are used for contacts?

7. What are competing regions doing to foster high-technology development? Are ideas promoted elsewhere worth imitating and improving?

The diagnosis will lead to the identification of "gaps" and opportunities. The objective is to document incubation, sponsorship, success models, business support, R&D activities, and venture capital for each one of the existing and emerging high-technology sectors. This will yield leverage points on which both government and business can implement supportive programs and focus their efforts. Naturally, the leverage points will be different for each region, depending on the existing infrastructure and the potentials of the high-technology sectors that thrive in the region. Targeting actions toward major gaps identified or toward high-technology sectors with high potential is likely to give coherence and focus to the strategy.

The development strategy is not an effort that is repeated every year. On the contrary, a sound diagnosis and a shared vision in terms of major action programs is likely to remain valid for a while. From time to time, corrections will be needed. Every economic development strategy needs refocusing after a few years of application, as internal and external conditions have changed.

A Strategy and an Implementation Program

The diagnosis has to go beyond analysis and lead to commitment to action. Unless there is agreement on the key elements of the diagnosis, controversies will arise and commitment to act will evaporate. Thus it is important that an effort be made to build a strong local consensus behind the diagnosis and the strategy that stems from it. With that purpose in mind, the strategy as an end-product will be composed of two distinct documents: the development strategy and a plan of action program.

The *development strategy* will propose a vision of what is actually feasible and the key leverage points to achieve this vision. The strategy will be presented in a document that will be widely distributed so as to build awareness of the promising high-technology sectors and of the weaknesses to be corrected. The institutional linkages and support systems that are needed to develop home-grown firms should also be addressed. However, the focus of the strategy has to be limited to a few visible factors that have high leverage potentials for the long-term/short-term considerations are valid only as a part of a coherent framework oriented toward the future.

A *plan of action programs* to develop linkages between small and large firms, to promote the visibility of successes, and to build momentum will need to be articulated for the short-term. Programs will focus on areas such as contract research, venture capital, initial contacts, and institutions to support entrepreneurs. Promoting the visibility of successes and building public support for needed changes are also important.

The following is a partial list of programs, both private and public, that can be implemented to bring about the development of a high-technology cluster from these two starting points.

Diffusing Information on Role Models. The diffusion of real and credible information about entreprenurial successes and failures in the local market and in national or international high-technology sectors is a very important aspect of implementation. The purpose is to provide accurate information to entrepreneurs who have decided to launch their businesses. It also aims at giving visibility to successes in the region.

The purpose is not to flatter egos or to emphasize short-term successes in a publicity campaign. On the contrary, the aim of these campaigns is to provide uncertainty-reducing information to entrepreneurs. Successful high-technology entrepreneurs can demonstrate, to all would-be imitators, the rewards and difficulties associated with high-technology start-ups. The visibility of successes and failures gives credibility and social support to entrepreneurial acts. It provides information that:

indicates the high-technology sector where entry is possible and local or national demand exists

shows the growth management problems that entrepreneurs have to face in product development, marketing channels, distribution outlets, personnel, and cash flow

tells the entrepreneurs about the requirements for designing a proper business plan and indicates the kinds of financing sources available to him

Multiplying Linkages for a Rich Environment. The development of a rich, local commercial environment in which large firms in the manufacturing service and financial sectors supply their needs by experimenting with local or newly created firms is the second type of program. Established firms within a region can contribute to triggering a process of high-technology development by buying from local start-ups, and offering them products or services.

Without intervention by private parties or a public–private partnership, linkages between large and small firms or between state-of-the-art research centers and businesses will tend to decrease, following the natural law of entropy. For instance, buyers will tend to meet supply needs from experienced sources that have provided good service in the past and where managers have developed good informal relationships with them. There is nothing wrong with such behavior, except that the possible external effects of innovative buying decisions are lost to the local economy. Successful researchers in universities also tend to become isolated from the "locals" and especially from local, small businesses that could access their newly developed technologies.

The multiplication of linkages within a community can be achieved by a number of mechanisms.

Innovative Buyers. An innovative buyers' program can be sponsored by a private association such as a High Technology Council or a Chamber of Commerce. Through this program, executives of large firms agree to set aside a proportion of their procurement expenditure for start-ups. Local procurement by established firms from start-ups or emerging firms should be strongly encouraged. Leadership by the management of mature firms (which are often several steps above actual procurement decision) can abate resistance to buying from new firms or from outside suppliers.

It is worth stressing that we are not proposing a "buy locally" campaign. Economic development is not really fostered because the local printing shop lands the annual calendar contract. What should be tossed on the local market are "problems" that require unique solutions. In particular, the granting of initial contracts to newly established manufacturing and services firms on the basis of personal track record of the founding teams requires personal commitment of a few innovative executives in positions of authority. Actual performance of such programs should be monitored, and public recognition should be given to achievements. Several firms have procurement programs that can serve as models. IBM has a worldwide program to assist local suppliers to bid on work anywhere in the IBM system.

Why should established firms engage in procurement from newly established suppliers? First, proximity of suppliers makes for speedy delivery and adjustment of specifications. Second, established firms will be able to rely on a responsive pool of suppliers to whom they can subcontract research as well as the manufacturing of components and parts. Third, procurement from emerging high-technology firms in the region will allow for rapid transfer of new technologies leading to increased productivity. Finally, procurement of products and services at the state-of-the-art level may allow the incorporation of technologies to develop competitive edges.

However, not all firms can become innovative buyers, only those with a reward system that recognizes risk-taking and not the tendency to cover one's position by relying on well-known established suppliers.

Information Networks. The development of information networks to connect buyers and entrepreneurs will enrich the possibilities of the environment. Entrepreneurs thrive on opportunities. Ensuring that entrepreneurs are exposed to local opportunities should be an important program. Private organizations, such as Chambers of Commerce or High Technology Councils, can sponsor activities that will lead to the development of networks. Subcontracting fairs expose small firms to the potential of large firms as customers, and vice-versa.

Local Subcontractors. Special task forces to promote local subcontracting and procurement of high-technology wares can also assist in the development of commercial links between emerging firms and established local firms.

Databases. A database of high-technology firms in the region that indicates the technical expertise available and kinds of products offered may also be useful. A number of firms have been founded to provide services of this nature to the venture capital industry. These data banks do not need to be very sophisticated, but they have to be user-friendly. A data bank of this sort is best designed and operated by a private group, due to the hesitancy of entrepreneurs to disclose such information to government organizations.

User Groups. User groups helps to promote linkages. Engineers and scientists are loyal to their own organization, but they are also interested in the emerging technologies of the day. Meetings that would otherwise be difficult to organize between suppliers and buyers are easy to set up around technical issues such as robotics, CAD/CAM, genetic engineering, expert systems, and artificial intelligence.

Industry–University Consortia. These can be fashioned to transfer state-of-the-art technologies from first-rate research centers to industry or to help universities get up to par with technologies used within leading technology-based businesses. The purpose of this type of exchange is basically to help universities stay attuned to local industry needs, particularly in terms of highly qualified manpower.

These formal mechanisms for multiplying linkages cannot be complete substitutes for the informal networks that are built between scientists and engineers interested in emerging technologies and between accountants, lawyers, and venture capitalists interested in the development of high-technology firms.

Maintaining Technical Effervescence. The quality of the technical inputs available in a region is highly dependent on the degree of technological effervescence in the area. R&D usually plays a major role in a development strategy. Yet, this role is often misunderstood. As a first step, a distinction must be made between basic research and applied R&D.

Basic Research. Locally conducted basic research is important in the long-run to maintain technological effervescence in the area. However, to be stimulative, basic research should be at the frontier of knowledge. In fact, some skeptics will argue that most basic research projects do not qualify. Money is not always the limiting factor. Good researchers tend to conglomerate around centers of excellence, and money does not necessarily buy excellence. Thus, private and public leaders in a region should ensure that basic research institutions are centers of excellence and remain so on a sustained basis.

Yet basic research will always be a passive factor in the development process. Most university professors and researchers are not entrepreneurs and never will be. Furthermore, the university is not a good incubator because it is too far from the marketplace. Universities should not attempt to usurp the role of incubators just because they have easier access to funds.

A distinction should be made between universities and technology institutes. A further distinction should be made between technology institutes that work at the frontier of R&D and those that do not. The role of universities is to train the mind and transmit knowledge. Technical institutes are concerned with the development of knowledge, particularly in professional and scientific areas. The major contribution that universities and technical institutes can make to the development of a region is to educate, transmit knowledge, and commit students to excellence. Moreover, professors, particularly in technical institutes, should be encouraged to develop links with the business community and with entrepreneurs, even if it is only to transmit entrepreneurial values to their students. Outside consulting should also be encouraged.

Here is a list of actions likely to maintain technical effervescence in basic research:

competing for federally funded centers of excellence in engineering

establishing university chairs and attracting leading scholars in selected fields targeted for development

monitoring and comparing the position of universities in the region with respect to federal, state, and industrial funding in select technical fields

ensuring a competitive level of funding for graduate education in a broad range of high-technology sectors

Applied Research. Applied R&D is a key factor in the start-up and clustering process. Applied R&D should be market driven, if it is to lead to entrepreneurial effervescence. Thus, the development strategy should ensure that public funds earmarked for R&D are channelled into profit seeking and preferably small firms with growth potential. To qualify as market driven, applied R&D should be conducted for profit-seeking purposes and be tied directly to potential market applications. Most applied R&D conducted in universities, government laboratories, and non-profit research centers does not qualify and thus rarely leads to technological entrepreneurship. The only efficient test for the marketability of an applied research project is whether a profit-seeking organization intimately tied with the marketplace is willing to fund in total, or in part, the R&D.

We recognize the political weight of researchers in non-profit institutions. The power of the "social benefits of innovation" argument is such that public funding of non-profit research organizations will continue for a long time. Policies should be implemented to increase the market potential of their research activities. Here are some measures that could be enacted:

1. Government initiated applied R&D should be contracted to profit-oriented firms, and preferably those with a business mission, instead of universities or other non-profit organizations.

2. Universities and other non-profit organizations bidding on government-funded applied-R&D projects should be encouraged (or forced) to team up with profit-seeking firms.

3. Government laboratories should subcontract to private firms a predetermined percentage of their applied R&D.

4. Defense and aerospace contractors should be encouraged to subcontract applied R&D to small firms.

Governments can also improve the efficiency funds allocated to research by privatizing public applied-R&D laboratories. The full or partial privatization of these laboratories could do much to instill priorities and activities that are effectively market driven. Privatization is often resisted on the basis that, under private leadership, these institutions would move out of the area: this is highly improbable. Complex organizations do not move out easily. In many regions, where high-technology firms are few, the privatization of applied research laboratories can be the cornerstone of a development strategy. The turbulence associated with the institutional change can turn these laboratories into good incubators.

Venture Capital. Venture capital flourishes in high-technology clusters, and can speed up the development process. A development strategy should ensure that the risk capital available ends up in "smart" hands. This is not always the case. Government-owned venture capital firms, and non-profit venture capital funds have, on the whole, a poor record in first-round financing. Venture capital firms sponsored by corporations do not also have the best of records for financing start-ups.

An effective development strategy should attempt to spawn a regional network of "financial entrepreneurs," oriented towards high-technology ventures. The promotion of a formal venture-capital industry as well as informal venture capital activities is critical.

Professional first round venture capitalists tend to invest close to their operating base, as they are quite involved in the management of the firms they invest in. The Boston region does not count more than ten "early stage" active venture capital firms in the high-technology area. Most regions can do with much less. Successful entrepreneurs will generate additional venture capital. Early-stage venture capitalists will weed out the bad ventures (sometimes getting burned in the process) and will assist the good ones up to later-stage financing. Good first-round venture capitalists can attract national and international capital for second stage financing. Thus, a region should not be overly concerned about second-round venture capital but focus policies towards stimulating first-round venture capital. Policies aimed at stimulating first-round venture capital can be tax oriented. Yet, the real lever is the joint decision by public leaders and the managers of financial institutions to channel funds to venture organizations, and more specifically, to venture capitalists who will experiment with start-ups and emerging firms.

Releasing informal venture capital depends partly on fiscal incentives. There is circumstantial evidence about the effect of taxation on the development of high-technology clusters. The most important items seem to be the capital gains tax and the marginal rate of personal taxation. A lowering of tax in these two areas seems to increase significantly the availability of risk capital. Tax incentives associated with R&D may also be useful, especially if they lead profitable firms to subcontract research. Emulation caused by success stories should not be underestimated as a trigger for informal venture capital. In the final analysis, the release of informal venture capital depends on the commitment of already successful entrepreneurs to economic development through high technology. A strategy should marshal the commitment of these former entrepreneurs.

However, technical entrepreneurs who have launched their firms with their own funds often wish to maintain the control of their firms and shy away from formal or informal venture capitalists. These entrepreneurs are afraid that venture capitalists will give preference to growth and expansion at the expense of their own entrepreneurial control. Public subsidies should not allow technical entrepreneurs to keep control of their firms at the expense of exploiting their full potential.

Many states and provinces have concluded that there is a lack of venture capital. Attention has been paid to generate alternative sources for equity investment in "seed funding," to prove a technology concept from a business viewpoint, and in "start-up financing," for further development and refinement prior to launching. Thus, several states have established state-funded venture-capital pools. A state venture-capital organization is usually funded from appropriations from the sale of revenue bonds. After examining proposals, grants are made to cover parts of product development costs. Loan guarantees, subordinated unsecured debt, and equity investment are made for the start-up situation. The criteria for investment are usually that jobs will be created in the area and that public investment is leveraged by private investments. Funded firms agree to pay royalties on sale of products and repay loans.

The Pennsylvania "challenge grants" for seed capital funds were established in 1984 under the Board of Ben Franklin Partnership Fund. The purpose was to attract private investments, which, together with state funds, were to be used to meet the capital needs of small businesses in their early stages of product or process development. The program was intended to fill a gap left by formal and private venture capital which is said to focus on larger and on later-stage financing. Four regional seed capital funds were set up under later-stage financing. Four regional seed capital funds were set up under this program. Each involved the participation of the regional "Advanced Technology Centers" as limited partners, representing the state's financial share.

The program is administered by the Ben Franklin Partnership Board appointed by the governor and the General Assembly. A professional fund manager is recommended by the regional Advanced Technology Center who acts as the state's financial agent and as the limited partner in the regional fund. State allocations came initially from Economic Revitalization Funds. General funds are now being used. The plan is to expend $750,000 for creation of each of four regional funds to be matched three-to-one by private money for a total of $12 million statewide. Returns are intended to be reinvested, each fund having a minimum life of seven years.

Pennsylvania small businesses can present proposals for product or process conceptualization, technical feasibility assessment, product development and refinement, and prototype development. All are activities eligible for financing. Investments are normally less than $250,000 and rarely exceed $500,000. Regional funds are required to maintain a balanced portfolio with regard to stages of business growth. Investments can be any combination of equity, royalty arrangements, and debt.

We have strong reservations with regard to these government-supported institutions. The major difficulties associated with the state venture-capital institutions is that they tend to attract high-risk proposals that will not be funded by the formal or informal venture capital sector, basically because they are not sound. Moreover, public venture-capital agencies have difficulty accessing the informal referral networks through which valuable information about prospective entrepreneurs flow. Third, public venture capital can be very active at the financing stage, but they tend to be less present in the active surveillance and in the provision of managerial support to funded enterprises. Fourth, they do not tend to attract good venture capitalists. Good venture capitalists are probably the best paid people in America. Very seldom will a publicly sponsored organization be able to offer them a competitive compensation package. Finally, state seed and start-up venture-capital funds tend to hinder the development of informal venture capital and the action of individual investors.

Institutional Supports for Entrepreneurs. Some entrepreneurs or small firms may benefit from business advice in the preparation of a business plan and in locating capital sources. A number of private organizations, university-related organizations, and public organizations can be set up to provide such services to entrepreneurs. They aim to provide services such as:

technology-transfer agreements and assistance in product development

marketing research to assess potential and technical advice on feasibility of projects

professional, legal, accounting, or technical assistance in designing plans or acquiring technology

training of entrepreneurs in product development, strategy development, and growth management

provision of low-rent incubator services

Private, non-profit institutional support to entrepreneurs can enlist the active contribution of existing business and former entrepreneurs. The MIT Enterprise Forum, the Minnesota Cooperation Office, and the University City Science Center are good examples. A private non-profit organization founded and supported by successful entrepreneurs, corporations, or foundations can assist entrepreneurs in building an appropriate business plan and drawing on community resources.

The planning, staffing, and financing of a contemplated business opportunity requires a sound business approach. By applying the knowledge, experience, and contacts of former entrepreneurs, opportunities can be assessed. Determination of the size of the opportunities, the uniqueness of the products or services, and the profitability of the venture can be made. Beyond the business plan, this private institutional support to entrepreneurs can draw on supporting organizations, contacts, and former entrepreneurs for advice, initial financing, and management support.

Public institutional support to entrepreneurs is premised, on the one hand, on the failures of formal and informal venture capitalists to fund proposals with a high social return, and on the other hand, on the communications difficulties that entrepreneurs experience in getting business advice and achieving product development. Given the highly uncertain returns, most of these institutional supports to entrepreneurs are state funded, and are operated as non-profit organizations. In some cases, private corporations or foundations also contribute funds, as a social responsibility action. These centers are normally affiliated with universities, particularly because such a location is deemed best to develop interactions with research facilities, public funding, venture capital, and professional business advice.

Public institutional support to entrepreneurs aims at transferring technology from university research laboratories to start-up firms. It exists to evaluate new product ideas, and to perform applied R&D to demonstrate commercial feasibility, and to diffuse technology to established small firms. Incubator facilities provide low rent for office or laboratory to entrepreneurs, with common services such as photocopying, legal advice, and computer access. Support and funding of R&D activities to help entrepreneurs develop product and prototypes, with a view toward early-stage commercialization are usually provided in technology centers affiliated with universities. Many innovation centers have been established with the purpose of evaluating the commercial viability of new product ideas or inventions.

The primary mission of the Institute For Ventures In New Technology (INVENT) is entrepreneurial assistance. The Institute is affiliated with Texas A&M University and was created by the Texas legislature in 1983. Its purpose is to provide technical assistance in the evaluation and development of new products and processes for small business enterprises and individual entrepreneurs. Its objectives are to make available the intellectual resources of the state's higher education system and to solicit, select, and research ideas and innovations that have high market potential.

The legislature empowered the Institute to own and transfer ownership interests, such as patent rights, royalties, and equity in the developing technology that it assists. INVENT is organized as a division of the Texas Engineering Experiment Station, a part of the Texas A&M University System.

The sources of ideas for initial screening by INVENT are expected to be Texas A&M faculty and students, individual inventors, small and large firms, and government agencies. The goal is to commercialize ten projects per year: the estimated survival rate from initial submission to actual start-up of a business is 2 percent. INVENT operates by identifying high-potential business ideas and helping the entrepreneur move his project to the point where it can be financed and started. INVENT uses the faculty and graduate students of Texas A&M and other Texas universities to perform product development and engineering, market analysis and planning, human resource analysis, financial planning, and the creation of a business plan. The entrepreneur is then introduced to sources of investment capital and assisted in negotiating. INVENT would receive a return from equity participation or from royalties. Items found not suitable for development by INVENT but with commercial potential are brokered to other organizations. The involvement of graduate students may yield future dividends as the entrepreneurial training of these individuals is certainly enhanced.

Conclusion

The successful introduction of a new technology usually implies much trial and error. Thus, a development strategy should aim at favoring experimentation by the multiplication of innovative but reality-grounded programs. Central Park was not made in one year. Trees take their time to grow and mature, no matter how much fertilizer is used. In a similar fashion, sound industrial policies can lead to an agglomeration of high-technology firms over the year, but the process has to be well understood before it can be managed.

The development of a high-technology cluster takes time. Decades are needed to build a few generations of high-technology firms that will become incubators and initial contractors. Only a strong sense of leadership can ensure such long-term commitments to a region. Thus, a strategy should aim at creating the permissive conditions for the creation and growth of firms.

Appendix

The data was gathered from the Business County partners published by the U.S. Census Bureau for 1971, 1974, 1977, 1980, and 1983. Counties forming each one of the metropolitan areas appear in table A–1.

The ten technological fields were defined using SIC codes. Table A–2 gives for each field the corresponding SIC codes used. The index of diversity was calculated using the following equation:

$$D = \sum_{i=1}^{x} Y_{RC} \log_{10} \frac{Y_{RC}}{1/10}$$

where   x = 10 technical fields
Y_{RC} = % of total in i^{th} technical field.

Table A–1
Geographic Agglomerations of High Technology

Metropolitan Area	Counties
Phoenix, AZ	Maricopa
Los Angeles, CA	Orange, Los Angeles, and San Bernadino
San Diego, CA	San Diego
Santa Clara/San Jose/San Francisco, CA	San Jose, Contra Costa, and San Francisco
New Haven/Stamford, CT	New Haven and Fairfield
Denver/Boulder, CO	Boulder, Denver, and Jefferson
Tampa, FL	Hillsborough and Pinellas
Atlanta, GA	Fulton and DeKalb
Chicago, IL	Cook, Lake, and Dupage
Lexington, KY	Fayette
Baltimore, MD/Washington, DC	Fairfax, VA; Montgomery, Prince Georges, and Baltimore, MD; and Washington, DC
Boston, MA	Middlesex, Norfolk, and Suffolk

Table A-1 continued

Metropolitan Area	Counties
Detroit, MI	Wayne, Ann Arbor, and Oakland
Minneapolis/St. Paul, MN	Ramsey and Hennepin
Kansas City, MO	Jackson
St. Louis, MO	St. Louis
Buffalo/Rochester, NY	Monroe and Erie
New York, NY	Bergen, Morris, Hudson, Middlesex, Essex, and Union, NJ; Rockland, Westchester, Richmond, New York, Bronx, Queens, Kings, Nassau, and Suffolk, NY
Albequerque/Santa Fe, NM	Bernalillo, Santa Fe, and Sandaval
Raleigh/Durham, NC	Wake, Orange, Durham, and Guilford
Columbus, OH	Franklin
Portland, OR	Multnomah, Washington, and Clackamas
Philadelphia, PA/Princeton, NJ	Philadelphia, Chester, Delaware, and Montgomery, PA; Camden and Mercer, NJ
Pittsburgh, PA	Allegheny
Austin, TX	Travis
Dallas/Fort Worth, TX	Dallas and Tarrant
Houston, TX	Harris
Salt Lake City, UT	Salt Lake, Davis, Provo, and Utah
Seattle, WA	King
Milwaukee, WI	Milwaukee and Waukesha

Table A–2
Ten Technical Fields and the Corresponding SIC Codes

Technical Field	SIC Code
Electronic components and instruments	367, 386
Defense and aerospace	348, 351, 372, 376
Pharmaceuticals, chemicals, and biotechnology	281, 282, 283
Software and data-processing services	737
Manufacturing technologies	381, 382
Communications	361, 362, 366
Biomedical and optical instruments	383, 384
Computers	357
Universities	822
R&D and professional services	891, 892, 7391

Bibliography

Armington, Catherine. 1984. *The changing geography of high technology businesses.* Washington, D.C.: Applied Systems Institute.

Birch, David L., and MacCracken, Susan. 1984. *The role played by high technology firms in job creation.* Cambridge, Mass.: MIT Program on Neighborhood and Regional Change.

Block, Zenas, and MacMillan, Ian C. 1985. *The paradox of new venture planning.* New York: New York University Center for Entrepreneurial Studies.

Block, Zenas. 1982. Can corporate venturing succeed? *The Journal of Business Strategy,* Vol. 3, No. 4, pp. 21–33.

Bollinger, Lynn, et al. 1983. A review of literature and hypotheses on new technology-based firms. *Research Policy.* Vol. 12, pp. 1–14.

Burgelman, Robert A. 1984. Managing the internal corporate venturing process. *Sloan Management Review,* Vol. 25, No. 1, pp. 33–48.

———. 1983. Corporate entrepreneurship and strategic management. *Management Science,* Vol. 29, No. 12, pp. 1349–1364.

———. 1983. A process model of internal corporate venturing in the large diversified firm. *Administrative Science Quarterly,* Vol. 28, pp. 223–242.

Cooper, Arnold C. 1970. *The founding of technologically-based firms.* Milwaukee, Wis.: The Center for Venture Management.

———. 1985. The role of incubator organizations in the founding of growth oriented firms. *Journal of Business Ventures,* Vol. 1, No. 1, pp. 75–86.

Fast, Norman D. 1976. The future of industrial new venture departments. *Industrial Marketing Management,* Vol. 8, pp. 264–273.

———. 1979. A visit to the new venture graveyard. *Research Management,* Vol. 22, No. 2, pp. 18–23.

Garven, David A. 1983. Spin-offs and the new firm formation process. *California Management Review,* vol. 25, No. 2, pp. 3–20.

Glassmeir, Amy K., et al. 1983. *Recent evidence on high technology industries' spatial tendencies.* Berkeley, Calif.: University of California, Institute of Urban Studies.

Jacobs, Jane. 1969. *The economy of cities.* New York: Random House.

Jacobs, Jane. 1984. *Cities and the wealth of nations.* New York: Random House.

Kanter, Rosabeth Moss. 1983. *The change masters.* New York: Simon and Schuster.

———. 1985. Supporting innovation and venture development in established companies. *Journal of Business Venturing,* Vol. 1, No. 1, pp. 47–60.

Malecki, Edward J. 1981. Product cycles, innovation cycles and regional economic change. *Technological Forecasting and Social Change,* Vol. 19, No. 1, pp. 291–306.

———. 1981. Science, technology and regional economic development. *Research Policy,* Vol. 10, pp. 312–334.

Mengsch, Gerhard. 1975. *Stalemate in technology.* Cambridge, Mass.: Harper and Row.

National Science Foundation. 1983. *The literature on the innovation process.* Washington, D.C.

Olleros, Xavier. 1984. *The process life cycle and technological competition.* Montreal: Ecole des Hautes Etudes Commerciales.

Porter, Michael. 1980. *Competitive strategy.* New York: Free Press.

———. 1985. *Competitive advantage.* New York: Free Press.

Quinn, James B. 1979. Technological innovation, entrepreneurship and strategy. *Sloan Management Review,* Vol. 20, pp. 19–20.

Roberts, Edward B. 1972. *Influences upon performance of new technical enterprises.* In A. Cooper and J. Komives, eds., *Technical entrepreneurship: A symposium.* Milwaukee, Wis.: The Center for Venture Management.

———. 1980. New ventures for corporate growth. *Harvard Business Review,* Vol. 59, No. 4, pp. 134–142.

Shapero, Albert. 1983. *The role of the financial institutions of a community in the formation effectiveness and expansion of innovating companies.* Columbus, Ohio: Shapero-Huffman Associates.

Schumpeter, Joseph A. 1934. *The theory of economic development.* Cambridge, Mass.: Harvard University Press.

Sirbu, Marvin, et al. 1976. *The formation of a technology-oriented complex.* Cambridge, Mass.: MIT Center for Policy Alternatives.

Stevenson, Howard. 1983. *A perspective on entrepreneurship.* Boston, Mass.: Harvard Business School.

U.S. Congress. 1984. *Technology, innovation and regional economic development.* Washington, D.C.: Office of Technology Assessment.

Utterback, James M., and Abernathy, William J. 1975. A dynamic model of process and product innovation. *Omega,* Vol. 3, pp. 639–656.

Vernon, Raymond. 1960. *Metropolis 1985.* Cambridge, Mass.: Harvard University Press.

Vinson, Robert, and Harrington, Paul, 1979. *Deepening high technology industries.* Boston, Mass.: Department of Manpower Development.

Von Hipple, Eric. 1977. Successful and failing internal corporate ventures: An empirical analysis. *Industrial Marketing Management,* Vol. 6, pp. 163–174.

Vesper, Karl H. 1984. Ten questions for corporate venture climate analysis. Working Paper. Seattle, Wash.: University of Washington School of Business.

———. 1984. Three faces of corporate entrepreneurship: A pilot study. Working Paper. Seattle, Wash.: University of Washington School of Business.

Index

About the Authors

Roger Miller is professor of technology and management at the University of Quebec in Montreal, Canada. He is also a founding partner of SECOR, Inc., a research and strategic analysis firm in Montreal. He holds degrees in engineering from Ecole Polytechnique (B.Sc.) and Stanford University (M.Sc.) as well as degrees in managerial economics from Columbia University (M.B.A.) and Université de Louvain (D.Sc.).

Professor Miller is engaged in research and consulting activities to integrate technology considerations in strategic planning. He has participated in three Royal Commissions in Canada, on (1) corporate concentration, (2) the newspaper publishing industry, and (3) financial and military project management. He was a Quebec Fellow at the Center for International Affairs at Harvard University and is presently a Research Fellow of the International Motor Vehicle Program at the Massachusetts Institute of Technology.

Marcel Côté is another founding partner of SECOR, as well as its present chairman of the board. He has twenty years of experience as a consultant in strategic analysis, economic development, and public policy. Over the years, Mr. Côté has been closely associated with a select number of high-technology firms to which he has provided consulting services and strategic analysis. He holds a B.Sc. from University of Ottawa and an M.Sc. from Carnegie-Mellon.

Mr. Côté's involvement in regional economic development dates back to his teaching career at the University of Sherbrooke. He was particularly involved in designing a development strategy for Canada's Beauce region, which has subsequently become a showcase for entrepreneurial-led regional economic growth. Mr. Côté is also a policy advisor to various governments. He is currently a Fellow at the Center for International Affairs at Harvard University.